The Language of the Gods in the World of Royal Ladies of Kerala. Toward the History of Women's Writing in Sanskrit in the 18th- to 20th-century Kerala

The Language of the Gods in the World of Royal Ladies of Kerala. Toward the History of Women's Writing in Sanskrit in the 18th- to 20th-century Kerala

Lidia Sudyka

Kraków 2019

Reviewed by:
Prof. Cezary Galewicz

Technical editor:
Marek Sudyka

Cover design:
Marta Jaszczuk
Cover photo:
Raja Ravi Varma, Lady with Veena, Wikimiedia Commons

Proofreading:
Ramon Shindler

The book was published thanks to the financial support of Faculty of Philology, Jagiellonian University.

ISBN 978-83-8138-089-8 (print)
ISBN 978-83-8138-355-4 (on-line, pdf)
https://doi.org/10.12797/9788381380898

Published in the e-book form plus paper copies.
The primary version of the book is the paper format.

Księgarnia Akademicka sp. z o.o.
31-008 Kraków, ul. św. Anny 6
e-mail: akademicka@akademicka.pl
https://akademicka.pl

Contents

Acknowledgements

The present monograph is a result of the project OPUS 4 2012/07/ B/HS2/01294 financed by the National Science Centre, Poland.

The title of my book obviously alludes to Sheldon Pollock's famous and voluminous *The Language of the Gods in the World of Men. Sanskrit, Culture, and Power in Premodern India.* My modest work acknowledges the presence of Kerala women in Sanskrit cosmopolis in premodern and modern times. It shows those "women who were not only articulate, but the script which they read was their own too" (Shah 2017: 80).

My gratitude is offered to the members of the poetesses' families, without whom it would not have been possible to present their biodata, their family background and, most importantly, their literary works. Special thanks go to Dr. R. P. Raja, who offered his vast knowledge of the culture and history of Kerala at my disposal. He was ready to answer all my questions and kindly organised my short stay in Punjar as well as a meeting with Srimati Chandravali Thampuran, belonging to the Royal Family of Cochin. But I would not have come to know Dr. R. P. Raja, had it not been for Sri Chemprol Raja Raja Varma. It was also he with whom I spoke for the first time about women writing in Kerala. He reacted immediately by inviting me to the Kowdiar Palace, where I was given a copy of the *Daśakumāracarita* written by his grandmother Ambadevi Tampuratti.

I have also collected many more debts of gratitude. These are Prof. Rajendran C., Prof. Cezary Galewicz, Dr. Kumuda Bayi,

Dr. Geethakumary K. K., Dr. E. K. Govinda Varma Raja, Dr. Maciej Karasiński, Ms. Agata Lenard, Mr. Ramon Shindler to whom I would like to thank. In fact, it would be a much longer list of people I would gladly mention, were it not for the lack of space. Still I hold them dear in my grateful memory.

To understand literary production, be it created by men or women, one needs historical and social background. Unfortunately, one can notice that pre-colonial Kerala is somehow neglected in the historiography of India. Dick Kooiman tries to provide an explanation for this fact noticing that 'the bewildering variety of numerous coastal kingdoms does not seem to offer the historian a solid base for the construction of more enduring frameworks." (Kooiman 1992: 587). Obviously, this or any other reason should not and does not exclude Kerala from historical perspective. The number of works on the pre-colonial and early colonial history of Kerala is steadily increasing,[1] although there are still deficiencies in this area. I have not devoted too much space to the history of kingdoms of Cochin (Mal. *kocci*), Travancore (Mal. *tiruvitāṅkōṭṭu˘, tiruvāṅkōṭṭu˘tiruvitāmkūṟ*) or the Zamorins of Calicut (Mal. *kōḻikkōṭu˘*; Kozhikode) as many authors have already concentrated on those issues. However, the history of the Kadattanad (Mal. *kaṭattanāṭu˘*) principality is not very well-known and researched, although the name of the realm and its rulers frequently appeared in English and French annals. Sometimes it is even difficult to connect all the names in the form given by French and English sources with this particular territory and its kings, and some authors are not ready to provide proper

[1] These are the works of M. G. S. Narayanan, Kesavan Veluthat, K. N. Ganesh, the recently published monograph on Ali Rajas by B. J. Mailaparambil (Mailaparambil 2012), a study of early colonial period by Margaret Frenz using Nicholas Dirks' concept of a 'little kingdom' (Frenz 2003), Hugo K. s'Jacob's analysis of Cochin political situation between 1663 and 1720 (s'Jacob 2001), and many other contributions to the subject.

explanations. Additionally, the same event of the Malabar[2] history in the 17th and 18th centuries will be described differently by English, French or other sources taking into consideration different attitudes and evaluations of their participants. Unfortunately, as for now, it seems that the point of view of Kadattanad *rājas* cannot be taken into account as no sources expressing their opinions on what happened and why during the most turbulent periods of their history have been preserved. From other sources we learn that they were very skilful players, and had to be, reigning over a very small principality but geographically located in the region of utmost interest for Europeans arriving in India. To deal with their enemies, they employed various strategies trying to protect their inheritance. They not only fought courageously against the local powers, then the Portuguese, but also negotiated with native kings or the English, the French or Mysore invaders. They periodically left their ancestral palaces and then came back. All of them had woven each his own thread into the magic fabric which is the history of the Malabar Coast kingdoms.

In contrast, the history of Punjar[3] *rājas* seems to be less tumultuous. The scion of Pandyas (Skt. *pāṇḍya*, Tam. *pāṇṭiyar)* who fled from Madurai (Tam. *maturai*) secured a more peaceful place for himself and his descendants. A place where life could be lived far from political tensions, one could assume. Of course, it would be misleading as the involvement in the region's history is unavoidable. The history of this family has been touched in very few sources. There is no detailed study on Punjar's history. That is why in the present monograph I devoted some space to explain at

[2] During the British domination in the region lasting 150 years, Kerala consisted of three parts: Malabar (Mal. *malabār*), i.e. the northern part of Kerala, which was a part of Madras Presidency, and the native states of Travancore and Cochin, formally independent upon separate bilateral treaties. In 1956 they were joined and formed a state known as Kerala (Mal. *kēraḷa*). See the map on Fig. 5, p. 83.

[3] Also Anglicized as Poonjar, Mal. *pūññāṟ*.

least their beginnings as told by the family, the places where they still live and the temples where they still worship their gods. The approach presented here owes much to the attitude of a microhistorian: narratives concerning small principalities, their rulers and the intellectuals of that period in the south of India, individuals' biographies and an attempt to reconstruct their *Alltagsgeschichte*. Much can also be gained by looking at their portraits and photos, if there are any. But the focus of this research is on Kerala women writers as objects of memory.

The profiles of some poetesses have already been presented in the form of concise articles published in journals. These are: 1. 2016. "Zapomniana poezja. Sanskrycka twórczość kobiet z rodu władców Koczinu" in *Przegląd Orientalistyczny* 1–2 (257–258), pp. 217–230; 2. 2018. "The *Santānagopāla* as a narrative opening up intimate spaces. Lakṣmī Tampurāṭṭi and her poem" in *Opening up Intimate Spaces: Women's Writing, Autobiography and Biography in South Asia in Cracow Indological Studies*, vol. 20, No 2., pp. 71–87; 3. 2018. "Kerala Women's Writing in Sanskrit. Ambādevi Tampurāṭṭi of Cemprol Koṭṭāraṁ—her life and literary oeuvre" in *Rocznik Orientalistyczny*. Vol. LXXI, No. 2, pp. 187–197; 4. (forthcoming). "In search of women's Sanskrit writings in Kerala" in: *Rivista degli Studi Orientali*. This last article, which appears simultaneously with my monograph, is a kind of summary of the activities undertaken so far under my project, although it does not close it. Its continuation would be advisable and necessary.

Note on Transliteration

A number of Malayalam and Sanskrit words are frequently used in this book. The Sanskrit terms and quotations are given according to IAST. As to the Malayalam I apply ISO http://self.gutenberg.org/articles/ISO_15919.

The names of contemporary Indian writers, scholars, etc. are given in the form as they themselves use nowadays, i.e. Romanized. The names of the Malayali authors from the past are given in ISO in brackets when they appear for the first time and then in their Anglicized form. The titles of Sanskrit works and their authors, mythological personages as well as Sanskrit literary terms, etc. are given in IAST. As far as Kerala geographical names are concerned I try to provide the name in ISO (e.g. Mal. *tiruvanantapuram*), also its Anglicized form introduced during the British presence in India (e.g. Trivandrum) is given and sometimes the Romanized version of Malayalam words that one can find in different sources nowadays (e.g. Thiruvananthapuram). Some words may appear both in their Anglicized form as well as in Sanskrit or Malayalam transliteration, e.g.: Kathakali and *kathakaḷi*, Brahmin and *brāhmaṇa*. They do not connote any conceptual difference.

I. Background

1. Introductory remarks

yasyāḥ svarūpam akhilam jñātuṃ brahmādayo 'pi na spaṣṭāḥ /
kāma-gavī sukavīnāṃ sā jayati sarasvatī devī //

keralyāḥ

Victory to the goddess Sarasvatī,
who is the cow of plenty to the great poets,
and whose real nature cannot be clearly known
in its entirety even by Brahmā and others.

Keralī

What is the best way to start a book or a poem if not with a hymn addressed to Sarasvatī, the goddess of learning? It was a usual practice in India but here the eulogy has a peculiar feature—it is attributed to Keralī, whose name not only betrays links with Kerala in South India, but first of all reveals the female gender of the writer. Unfortunately, no further information has been preserved about the authoress, her verse found in Veṇīdatta's *Padyaveṇī*[4] and repeated in Jatindra Bimal Chaudhuri's anthology of Sanskrit verses attributed to Indian poetesses (Chaudhari 2001 vol. I: 15, transl. 81).

[4] *Padyaveṇī* is an anthology containing 889 verses ascribed to different poets. According to Aufrecht it was composed in 1644. The author, Veṇīdatta, introduced himself as a son of Jogajīvena and a grandson of Nīlakaṇṭha (Sternbach 1974: 28).

The present book focuses on Kerala women's writings in Sanskrit, an interesting and significant subject, yet hardly researched in Indology so far. Among the very few publications on the topic, we can find "Contribution of Kerala to Sanskrit Literature" written by Kunjunni Raja. The book itself is fairly informative, yet as regards to women writers it mentions only a handful of names and just a few titles of their compositions and as a rule it does not give any detailed information about their lives and works. Similarly, S. Venkatasubramonia Iyer, in his "Kerala Sanskrit Literature. A Bibliography", published in 1976, refers to women writers only six times. Considering such limited participation of women in literary creativity in Sanskrit, one can wonder whether we get its real picture indeed.

The famous spiritual master of the 19th century Swami Vivekananda, while travelling all over India and visiting Malabar, noticed, with perhaps utmost admiration, an astonishing fact that women in that region could speak Sanskrit. "When I myself was in that country, I met many women who spoke good Sanskrit, while in the rest of India not one woman in a million can speak it", he commented (Swami Vivekananda 1989: VII. 52).

It is an undeniable fact that the ability to speak Sanskrit must have entailed the ability to compose literary works in it. Although their compositions have not been made known to a wider public, be it for the lack of recognition for women as such and the reception of their oeuvre limited only to family circles or, if they had become true Sanskrit scholars, the lack of pupils who could take care of their *gurvīs*' fame, still it is possible to find traces of their literary activities in rare copies of forgotten publications or the vast abyss of family archives and glimpses of their life in the memory of their relatives.

Women's voices were not strong enough to spread widely through the ages, however, it is apparent that we cannot consider the history of Sanskrit literature as well as the picture of Indian society as complete without taking women's writing into account.

Kerala women's literary creativity will be treated here as a part of the cultural process showing the specificity and rank of Sanskrit literature in the South of India. Thus, the right point to start our investigations would be Sanskrit education in Kerala. The historical and cultural background of the region will be taken into consideration. Then the biographies of the authoresses will be provided and their oeuvre will be discussed.

The time span covered in the present monograph encompasses the 18th up to the beginning of the 20th century. The 18th century brought a lot of political, social and economic changes in the region. The politics of Martanda Varma (Mal. *mārtāṇṭavarma;* r. 1729–1758) in Travancore and Saktan Tampuran (*śaktan tampurān;* r. 1790–1805) in Cochin caused a break-up of the old feudal system, reducing the power of *nāyar*[5] chieftains and *nampūtiri*[6] landlords and gave grounds to the rise of strong centralised monarchies.[7] The royal courts in both kingdoms became influential centres of learning and arts and it seems only natural that the better possibilities of education for the women of these royal families and their way of life more open to the outer world[8] could make them aspire to the position and fame as Sanskrit scholars and poetesses, at least in the royal or family circles. Their situation was quite different than that of thousands of anonymous Keralan women writers developing their literary skills in the seclusion of their houses themselves and in fact for themselves. There are also

---

[5] Mal. *nāyar* (Anglicized as Nair, Nayar): 1) honorific plural from Mal. *nāyakan* (Skt. *nāyaka*), i.e. a leader, 2) the *śūdras* of Kerala, 3) Keralan soldiers of all castes.

[6] Mal. *nampūtiri* (Anglicized as Namputhiri, Nambudiri or Namboodiri)—a high strata of Malayali Brahmins (Skt. *brāhmaṇa*).

[7] Read more about state-building strategies in: Bayly 1984 and de Lannoy 1997.

[8] As Gianna Pomata notices: "At the court, the boundaries between the public and the private, the political and personal, had little significance indeed" (Pomata 1993: 16). And this statement is also valid for India.

better chances that at least some part of literary oeuvre of royal poetesses has been preserved by their families proud of their talent and education. That is why this research concentrated on the contribution of royal ladies to Sanskrit literature of Kerala. It should also be mentioned that these families were matrilineal and as K. Saradamoni notices, summing up her research on transformation of matrilineal society in twentieth century Travancore, "Matriliny, when compared to patriliny, gave women some amount of autonomy (...)" (Saradamoni 1999: 15). Before entering the subject of royal women writings, some issues pertaining to the social and community customs should be explained.

2. A few words on the Keralan society structure

The region of Kerala[9] is a narrow piece of land between the Western Ghats and the Arabian Sea, isolated by its geographical features from the rest of India, which, on the one hand, made the external communication difficult, and, on the other, created a special ambience to develop a very specific culture and helped in protecting it. The early history of the region is poorly documented.[10] The Cheras (Tam./Mal. *cēra*, Skt. *cera*) or Cēramāṉ Perumāḷs, as they use such a royal title, brought unity to this territory but due to the wars with Chola kings (Tam. *cōḻa*, Skt. *cola*), they lost their power in the 11th century and finally disappeared from the scene in the 12th century.[11] Their local vassals proclaimed

[9] William Logan, for many years Collector of the Malabar District and the author of voluminous compendium *Malabar*, when for the first time reached Kerala in 1864, noticed that this land where people speak the Malayalam language is also called Malayalam (Mal. *malayāḷaṃ*) or Keralam (Mal. *kēraḷaṃ*) (Logan 1981: 1).

[10] More about the Iron Age in South India in Sudyka 2014.

[11] More about Cēramāṉ Perumāḷs of Makōtai in Narayanan 1996.

themselves independent rulers. Afterwards, as Robin Jeffrey explains:

> For the next six or seven hundred years, dozens of petty chiefs waged intermittent wars. The largest and most successful of these rulers claimed Kshatriya status, but it seems likely that they were Nairs who as a result of political and military success were able to engineer a promotion in ritual status.
> (*Jeffrey 1994: 1*)

> Though a common culture overlay Kerala like a quilt thrown over cushions, the region that Vasco da Gama reached in 1498 was divided into as many as 90 petty principalities.
> (*Jeffrey 1992: 19*)

Those local rulers closely connected with a few great land-controlling families of Nambudiri Brahmins. As M. G. S. Narayanan explains, some of the feudatories of the Cheras were recognised as Kshatriyas (Skt. *kṣatriya*) and as such employed the suffix -*varma*[12] to their names. These were families of ancient chieftains

> (...) like those of Kōlattunāṭu, Puṟaikiḻānāṭu and Kuṟumpoṟa-ināṭu, who acknowledged the Cēra supremacy, (...) and the families of the new chieftains like the governors of Ēṟanāṭu, Vaḷḷuvanāṭu, Vempalanāṭu, Kīḻimalanāṭu and Vēnāṭu were treated as *sāmantas* [i.e. vassals-LS] during this age.
> (*Narayanan 1996: 150*)

Some of the old lineages achieved the *kṣatriya* status later on, after the disappearance of the Cheras from the scene. M. G. S. Narayanan explains the process of introducing the *kṣatriya varṇa* into the structure of South Indian society as follows:

> The tendency on the part of the kings to adopt the caste symbols and legendary claims of the northern rulers, and the readiness on the part of the Brahmin priesthood to confer such honours, would signify close co-operation between kings and Brahmins. Recruit-

[12] Skt. *varman*—shelter, defence protection.

> ment of the traditional rulers of Dravidian origin into the *Kshatriya* caste represents a definite stage in the progress of Aryanisation of South India. According to orthodox Brahminical theory it was the duty of a *Kshatriya* to the cow and the Brahmin and uphold *dharma*. In historical terms it meant the propagation of the caste system and the Hindu religion. Therefore the recruits to Kshatriya-hood were committed to the patronage of Aryan Brahmins and the promotion of Aryan culture. When kings began to take pride in their *Kshatriya* lineage, it reflected not merely the status they had already acquired in society, but also the part they wanted to play and their whole outlook on life. They naturally became champions of the cāturvarṇya and patrons of temples, Brahmins, and Sanskrit literature.
> (*Narayanan 1996: 81*)

Some royal houses like those of Vettatunad (Mal. *veṭṭatunāṭu˘*), Parappanad (Mal. *parappanāṭu˘*), Kurumpuranad (Mal. *kurum-puranāṭu˘*), Nedumpuranad (Mal. *neḍumpuranāṭu˘*) and the kings of Venad (Mal. *vēnāṭu˘*) claim their descendance from the Puraya branch of the Chera dynasty, whereas the Perumpadappu (Mal. *perumpaṭappu*) family considers themselves to be descendants of the Cheras of Makotai (Mal. *mākōtai*), a place identified as a neighbourhood of today's Kodungallur (Mal. *koṭuṅṅallūr*; Anglicized form Cranganore). Other ruling families belonged to the *brāhmaṇa* caste[13] and yet some others, such as the Zamorins[14] of Calicut, were considered lower in status to Brahmins and Kshatriyas.[15] The Zamorin, one of the most powerful sovereigns by

[13] These are the rulers of Chempakacherry (Mal. *cempakaśśēri*) and Edappally (Mal. *eṭappaḷḷi*).

[14] Zamorin (Mal. *sāmūtiri, sāmūri, tāmātiri, tāmūri*)—the title of a Hindu king ruling his kingdom from Calicut. The title of *zāmorin* might be the Arab form of Malayalam word *tampurān* (Narayanan 1996: 96–97) although some others connect the word to Sanskrit *samudra*—ocean.

[15] M. G. S. Narayanan explains: "(...) sāmantas who were not admitted into the Kshatriya fold for purposes of interdinning and intermarriage, and who considered themselves higher than the nāyars on account of their kingship,

the end of the 14th century, was considered not fit for presiding over *māmāṅkam*, a pan-Kerala assembly held at Tirunavaya (Mal. *tirunāvāya*) every twelve years, as he was not a Kshatriya (Ibrahimkunju 2007: 34). The only Muslim Royal Family of Kerala ruled from Cannanore (Mal. *kaṇṇanūr/kaṇṇūr*).[16] These medieval chiefdoms and kingdoms were highly militarised with a big warrior population and prominent martial culture. The most important share in this martial culture is attributed to the Nayar caste group,[17] although other communities, which is a less kown fact, were by no means devoid of it, as for instance the Nambudiri Brahmins or, more importantly, St. Thomas Christians (Bayly 1984: 182).

As far as literary traditions are concerned, Sanskrit was the main language of scholarship as well as of belles-lettres for many centuries. This is another factor shared by all these bigger and smaller kingdoms and chiefdoms, unifying the region which produced so many versatile Sanskrit scholars and writers, whose works are still venerated and known by heart by many Keralites. That is the case of the *Nārāyaṇīyam* of the famous Melpputtur Narayana Bhatta (16th/17th c. Mal. *mēlpputtūr nārāyaṇa bhaṭṭa*) and many other works.

A lot has been written about the matrilineal system of inheritance and about marriage customs among certain communities of Kerala. As C. J. Fuller writes, almost every visitor to Kerala eagerly commented on these habits.[18] The Nambudiri Brahmins

---

formed a sub-caste, in between the two, though there was no sanction for it in the old scripture" (Narayanan 1996: 150).

[16] Interestingly enough, this Muslim ruling house observed the matrilineal system of inheritance (Menon 2006: 214).

[17] For an extensive bibliography on the Nayars, see Fuller 1976.

[18] See accounts written by Duarte Barbosa, a Portuguese, who after spending several years on the Malabar Coast could speak Malayalam and in 1518 returned to Lisbon, or another Portuguese, Luís Vaz de Camões, who in his *Lusiads* also mentions Nayars and their habits. For more about the travellers

maintained their patrilineal system with the eldest son of the family marrying Antarjanam,[19] a woman from his own community, and their children were successors of the family. The younger brothers got into relationships (Mal. *sambandhaṃ*) with Nayar women[20] as the matrilineal system among this stratum of society turned out to be complementary for the economic needs of the Nambudiris. Nayar women were allowed to form unions with Brahmins. In general opinion a woman consorting with a man of a higher class purified the blood and raised the social status of her family. The progeny from such a marital relation belonged to their mother's caste and family and could not be treated as their father's heirs. The children stayed in their mother's taravad[21] or joint family, observing the matrilineal system of inheritance (Mal. *marumakkattāyaṃ*), whereby property was passed from a man to his sister's son. However, it was a senior male member of the family, called *kāraṇavan* (Mal.), who was responsible for the menagement of the taravad's property. Nothing could be done in the taravad without his knowledge. As Filippo Osella and Caroline Osella write:

> Hypergamous *sambandham* unions with Brahman permitted 'refinement' of the tharavadu, children born to such unions embodying qualities relatively superior to those of their mother and mother's brother. This betterment had obvious status repercussions.
> (*Osella & Osella 2000: 83*)

informing about the matrilineal inheritance, see Fuller 1974: 2–6 and Uyl den 1995: 72–74. About Camões, see Pierdominici Leão 2019.

[19] Mal. *antarjanam*, Skt. *antar-jana*—i.e. "a person [confined to] indoors", a title of a Nambudiri woman.

[20] There were subdivisions among the Nayars, and in the case of Nambudiri-Nayar marital relationships the higher subcaste was meant, the noblity of the country.

[21] Mal. *taṟavātŭ* = joint family observing the matrilineal system of inheritance (*marumakāttayam*). Originally the word indicated the territory under the authority of a particular family (Nair 2013: 68).

Of course such a system of social mobility could be and was used for different purposes. In general, the interest to keep it this way was on both sides, i.e. Brahmins and Nayars, although such an organization of family life also caused problems and pain for individuals.

Such a social practice had one important consequence: a Brahmin could not bring his wife and children to his ancestral house (Mal. *mana* or *illaṃ*) because the Nambudiris could live only with the members of their own caste. She with their children should stay in her mother's house, visited by her husband. A Nambudiri father could not "touch his own children with his *nāyar* consort without bathing afterwards to remove the pollution" (Fawcett 1901: 225).

The upbringing of children and all the household chores were shared by women of the taravad, who enjoyed considerable freedom. Kathleen Gough, who studied the Nayars, presented us with such a picture of a young Nayar woman's life:

> Through the day they took turns visiting the village bathing pool in couples, an event which gave them opportunity for gossip and allowed them to be seen by (although not converse with) the men of neighbouring groups. Old women proudly distributed the *taṟavāṭu*'s jointly owned jewellery among the young and marriageable women, helped them to apply cosmetics and to dress their hair, and obtained a vicarious satisfaction from their marital conquests. For a few years—until she had several children—a young woman's life was gay and not overburdened with work.
> (*Gough 1974: 356*)

Such scenes are also depicted in one of the first Malayali novels *Indulēkha*[22] by Chandu O. Menon (Mal. *cantūmēnōn*; 1847–1899).

---

[22] Indulēkha is the name of the heroine of this novel published in 1889. It was not the first novel written in Malayalam but the first one to win recognition and popularity as well as bringing fame to its author. The book sold out in three months and its first English translation was ready a year later (Tharu 2013: IX).

Definitely, Kerala women, excluding Nambudiri womenfolk, Antarjanams, had more influence over their own lives than in other parts of India. As Robin Jeffrey observes, in eighteenth-century America a woman had no control not only over her money and land brought into marriage, but actually even her clothes did not belong to her. At exactly the same time, Nayar women living in their joint families could be owners of properties[23] and the absence of daughters was disastrous for a family. As A. Sri Narayana Thampi, a Nayar aristocratic, wrote in 1905, in his family all the properties were in his mother's name. However, it is worth remembering that according to some legal texts, such as the 16th- or 17th-century CE *dharmaśāstra* text from Kerala entitled *Laghudharmaprakāśikā*, it seems that matrilineal kinship in medieval Kerala was "merely a mode of reckoning inheritance among males" (Davis, Jr. 2013: 154). The Kshatriyas of Kerala practised the habit of *anuloma* marriages, i.e. a woman was permitted to marry a man higher in the social scale. There were different Kshatriya families of Kerala whose daughters were married exclusively to Nambudiri Brahmins. However, the Royal Family of Travancore followed another custom. Its daughters were wedded to Kshatriyas belonging to a class called Koyil Tampurans (Mal. *kōyil*[24] *tampurān*) or Koil Pantalas (Mal. *kōyil panṭala*).[25] In Koyil Tampurans' (for a woman the proper title is Tampuratti [Mal. *tampurāṭṭi*]) families again the girls were always married to Nambudiri Brahmins. On the other hand, the male members of the Royal Travancore Family

[23] More about women's property rights in Kerala in Mukund 1999.

[24] The word *kōil* or *kōyil* is used in the sense of a palace or a Kshatriya prince.

[25] In *The Travancore State Manual* (Aiya 1906 II: 319) ten families of Travancorean Koyil Tampurans are named: from Kilimanur (Mal. *kiḷimānūr*), Changanacherry, Mal. *caṅṅanāśśēri*), Anantapuram (Mal. *anantapuraṃ*), Pallam (Mal. *pallaṃ*), Chemprol (Mal. *cemprōl*), Gramam (Mal. *gramaṃ*), Paliyakkara (Mal. *pāliyakkaṟa*), Karama and Vadakkematom (Mal. *vaṭakkemataṃ*).

used to marry Nayar girls. There were, however, certain limitations, namely the king could marry only a member of Amma Vidu (Mal. *ammavīṭŭ*, i.e.: "the house of a royal spouse"). These were the families in which the daughters were married to a king in the past and their male members had the title of Tambi (Tam. *tampi*) and female members that of Tankachi (Tam. *taṅkacci*).[26] Thus, in theory, a king could marry only a Tankachi but there was a way to escape this custom. A Nayar girl who was not a Tankachi could be adopted by a certain Amma Vidu. And the cases of such adoptions were recorded in the royal writs (Raja 2006: 234–236). Nevertheless, as it was an inter-caste marriage, again the children of the actual king could not inherit their father's throne, what is more, they were not even members of the royal family, just blood relatives. That is, only the progeny of female members of the royal family belonged to the Kshatriya caste and were considered as royal blood with rights to the throne and inheritance.

Many of the royal families followed the practises of using the same set of names among the family members. But what distinguishes one Rama Varma from the other bearing the same name is his birth star put before the name or his pet name, if he had such, added at the end.

That system of marriages in the case of the Nambudiris resulted in the creation of a class of intellectuals who could devote their full time and energy to cultural activities because they did not have any responsibilities. Their union with non-Brahmanic families again brought its fruit:

> All this helped the promotion of Sanskrit studies. Sanskrit entered the fabrics of all Varṇas in Kerala. This special phenomenon greatly helped the enrichment of Sanskrit learning in Kerala.
> (*Subramanian 2008: 10*)

[26] In the Tamil language *tampi* and *taṅkacci* mean a younger brother and a younger sister.

3. Education in Kerala in pre-modern times up to the 20th century

A child's basic education, namely writing, reading and counting, usually began at the age of four or five. Education was included in the code of conduct related to family life or *parivārikadharma*. The stages in the development of an individual were marked by spiritual ceremonies to follow in order and at a specific time; as Dr. R. P. Raja stated "harmonious and appropriate development of each and every member of a family ensured its sustenance and prevented it from disintegration".[27] In India initiation into the primary stage of education was and is still marked by the ceremony called *vidyārambha* (literally, "the beginning of learning") and at least in Kerala concerns children who have turned three, but are no more than five years old. *Vidyārambha* in Kerala is connected with the Navaratri (Skt. *navarātri*) festival, concluding in the Sarasvatī *pūjā* ceremony. As Sarasvatī is a goddess of learning, it is the most proper time to introduce a new adept into the educational process. Descriptions of these ceremonies can be found in memoirs, autobiographies,[28] or one see them today, collectively performed for a large number of children. The master of the ceremony, very often a teacher, writes letters and/or a *mantra* bringing the blessing of Sarasvatī and Gaṇapati, patrons of science and arts—*hariḥ śrīgaṇapataye namaḥ*—on the tongue of the child subjected to the ritual with a gold coin or a ring. Then a teacher takes the hand of a future pupil and makes the child write the same *mantra*/letters of the alphabet in spread-out rice, symbolizing the fact that acquiring knowledge leads to prosperity. Learning the script is an introduction to studying literature. During the ceremony the 51 letters of the Malayalam script are written but in the past, besides reading and writing in Malayalam, the stress was

[27] Personal communication on 22.01.2014.

[28] Wood 1985: 28–29, 44.

put on education in Sanskrit. The knowledge of the 'language of gods' was a must for the castes connected with Hindu temples, for others, such as for instance the Nayars, a nobilitating factor.

Normally, a teacher would start the teaching process with the *Siddharūpam*—a Sanskrit grammar composed in verse, still used in Kerala as the first textbook of Sanskrit.[29] The *Bālaprabodha* ("Instructions for the young") in Malayalam verse was also used. The *Samāsacakram* was a good introduction into word-compounds and the *Amarakośa*[30] developed a young adept's lexis. It was a matter of a few months to master the *Siddharūpam* but learning by heart the *Amarakośa* could take approximately one year. A teacher (Skt. *guru* ; Mal. *āśān*) recited the verses and the pupil (*śiṣya*) repeated them. And so every day until the student mastered the text. It was not a mental effort for a child, more physical, mechanical repetition, which trained the ability to memorize. Such memorization could be enjoyed by a child as a kind of game. This was not a child's first encounter with Sanskrit because from an early age, from his or her mother, aunts and grandmothers, he or she could get acquainted with and learn Sanskrit prayers and hymns. It can be expected that a four-year-old was able to recite from 30 to 40 Sanskrit verses. After some time the process of learning Sanskrit could give sheer enjoyment and satisfaction—the disciple was able to understand what he or she repeated day by day. After mastering grammar and vocabulary, the pupil was prepared to enter the *kāvyapāṭha*, i.e. studying classical Sanskrit literature. The first step was traditionally connected with learning the po-

[29] This grammar of Sanskrit inspired the Jesuit Johann Ernst Hanxleden (1681–1732) to present a description of Sanskrit based on it, and this work attracted the attention of the Croatian Carmelite Father Paulinus a Sancto Bartholomaeo (1748–1806), who, after his return from India, published *Sidharubam seu Grammatica Samscrdamica, cui accedit Dissertatio historicocritica in Linguam Samscrdamicam.*

[30] The popular name for the *Nāmaliṅgānuśāsana* ("Instructions concerning nouns and gender") composed by Amarasiṃha (c. 400 CE).

ems of Kālidāsa: *Meghadūta*, *Kumārasambhava* and *Raghuvaṁśa*, considered to be easy to remember and that is why labelled as the *laghutrayī*, literally "the light/simple trio". Then the young student was prepared to study the so-called *bṛhattrayī*, i.e. "heavy trio", namely the *Kiratārjunīya* of Bhāravi, the *Śisupālavadha* of Māgha and the *Naiṣadhacarita* of Harṣa. The whole process could take approximately four years. The selection of poems to study could also be different.[31] The excerpts from the *Ātmakatha* ("Autobiography") of K. V. Mussatu (Mal. *mūssatŭ*) quoted in the English translation by Ananda Wood (Wood: 44–65), describe K. V. Mussatu's Sanskrit education, and among the works taught by his teacher there were the *Śrī Rāmodantam*, the *Śrī Kṛṣṇavilāsam* and the *Raghuvaṁśa*. His father demanded that his son would be taught the *Māgham*, i. e. the poem of Māgha (c. 8th cent. CE), but the teacher did not have the book and could not obtain any copy. That was why the father stopped his son's lessons for several months.

There was an established pattern to analize each verse:

> The order in which a verse lesson proceeds is of course *ślōkam* (reciting the verse itself), *padacchēdam* (splitting the continuous line of verse into words), *vibhakti* (identifying the inflection of each word), *ākāmkṣa* (identifying the relations between the inflected words), *anvayam* (putting the words of the verse into a standard 'prose' order that emphasizes the relations between words and makes it easy to pick out the meaning), *anvayarttham* (reciting the re-ordered sentence with Malayalam terminations of grammar but with the same Sanskrit vocabulary), *paribhāṣa* (substituting Malayalam equivalents for the Sanskrit words and hence arriving at a formal Malayalam translation of the verse), and *sāram* (an informal explanation and commentary by the teacher on the meaning and significance of the verse).
> (*Wood 1985: 50*)

[31] See the selection of texts used in Sanskrit education of A. R. Rajaraja Varma (Mal. *rājarājavarma*; 1863–1918) as given in Subramanian 2008: 23–24. About A. R. Rajaraja Varma, see also Cielas 2016.

The higher level of education could begin after the *upanāyana*, meant as bringing someone (*upa* + *nī*) to the knowledge, skipping any other connotations of the term. And that meant education in the *gurukula* system, i.e. in the teacher's home or temple *maṭhas*, and with the stress on the *Vedas* in the case of Brahmin students, and education in specific *śāstras* for the others. At this point we are approaching the issue of women's education. The *vidyārambha* ceremony opened the way to education for a female child, the *upanāyana* was not available for the girls of Kerala. It goes without saying that one could not even imagine that the girls from Brahmin, Kshatriya or Samanta[32] families would attend a village school (*eḻuttupaḷḷi*—primary school, *paḷḷikuttam*—other schools[33]), let alone live in the teacher's home! However, in the case of aristocratic families, the instruction of children was conducted at home. A carefully selected teacher lived on the estate of the employer and taught all the children together, regardless of gender (see the photos and plans of the Chemprol and Kilimanur Palaces with a note showing the room of a teacher; Figs 1–2, pp. 30–31).

Teachers usually belonged to the Variyar (Mal. *vāriyar*) or Pisharoti (Mal. *piṣāroṭi*) subcaste. The Variyars, an important subcaste of the Ambalavasis,[34] resemble in many respects that of the Pisharotis, but they are Shivaites whereas the Pisharotis are Vaishnavas. The Pisharotis and Variyars' occupation was temple

[32] Mal. *sāmantan*—1) the chief of a district, 2) a son of a Brahmin born of a Kshatriya mother.

[33] The word *paḷḷi* meaning a non-Hindu shrine attests to the influence of Buddhism and Jainism on education in Kerala. There were also *kaḷaris* meant for physical education for training boys as well as girls (Mathew 1979: 53–56).

[34] Mal. *ampalavāsi*, lit. "one who lives in the temple" is applied to a caste whose occupation is temple service. In the social order they are situated between *brāhmaṇas* and *kṣatriyas*, on the one hand, and *śūdras* on the other, i.e. they belong to *antaralajāti* (intermediate castes). More on the Ambalavasis in Padmanabha Menon 1993: 146–161.

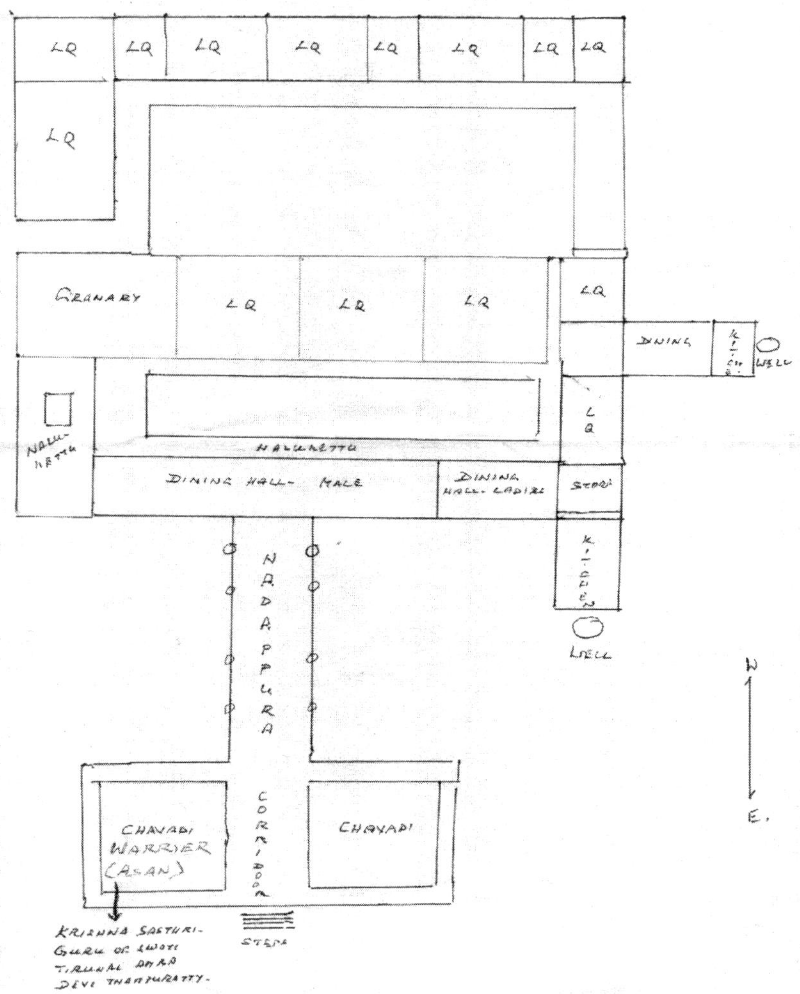

Fig. 1. Plan of the Chemprol Kottaram, Haripad.

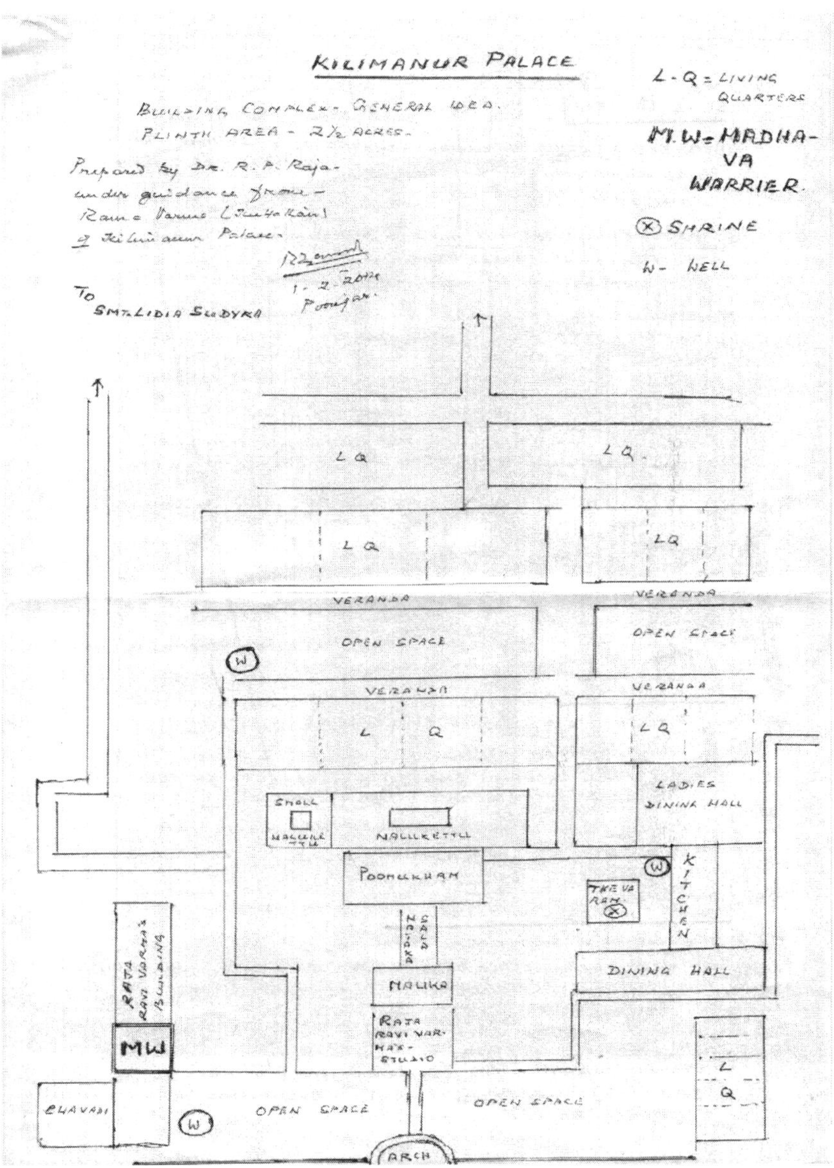

Fig. 2. Plan of the Kilimanur Palace prepared by Dr. R. P. Raja under the guidance of Rama Varma of the Kilimanur Palace.

service, namely cleaning it and supplying with flowers and garlands as well as assisting the Brahmin priest. The Pisharotis can act as they own priests. As they were well educated in Sanskrit,[35] they were appointed to teach Sanskrit in aristocratic families. The teacher, who usually lived on a Nambudiris' or Nayars' estate, participated in the life of this community. Thus, in addition to regular lessons, there were other opportunities to learn Sanskrit. The late C. K. Ravi Varma (1917–2011), a former diplomat and head of the aristocratic family (Mal. *kāraṇavan*) from the Chemprol Palace,[36] when asked about the education of girls in his family, described the following picture: his older sister, Asvati Nal[37] Srimati Tampuratti (Mal. *aśvati nāḻ śrimatī tampurāṭṭi*), called Kunjikutti (Mal. *kuññikuṭṭi*) (1915–1990), recites Pāṇini's grammar rules, and their teacher, helping in the kitchen, just grinds the coconut pulp and at the same time corrects the student. Asvati Nal Srimati, when she grew up, authored minor works in Sanskrit, unfortunately not preserved by the family, although there are anecdotes about the circumstances in which some of them were created. The old gentleman did not remember precisely how old his sister might have been at that time.[38]

Generally, a girl's education ended at the time when she became *puṣpavatī* (Skt. literally: "blooming; a menstruating woman"). At that moment radical changes occurred in the life of a young woman from the Nambudiri community. From that moment on she indeed was a person living behind doors. For those young

---

[35] Some of the Variyars were experts in astrology and astronomy. Tṛkkuṭaveli Śaṅkara Vāriyar's (c. 1500–1560) contribution to Indian astronomy and mathematics is worth paying attention (Unnithiri 2004: 207–211).

[36] I met Sri C. K. Ravi Varma in November 2006 while visiting Chemprol Kottaram (Mal. *koṭṭāraṃ*: 1. a royal residence, especially in Travancore; 2. a kind of temple office).

[37] Mal. *aśvati*, Skt. *aśvinī*—the first of 28 lunar mansions; Mal. *nāḻ*—a birth star.

[38] From interview notes taken on November 18, 2006.

girls the doors to the outer world closed along with the arrival of menstruation. Their education was finished. However, as was said above, the situation of a Nayar female aristocrat was different. She could develop in such a way as was shown in the novel *Indulēkha* but, most importantly, as is known from biographies, autobiographies and memories of my informants.

It should also be said that Sanskrit education in Kerala sometimes reached the lower strata of society: not only *śūdras*, but also the castes standing outside the *varṇa* system (i.e. Skt. *avarṇa*), such as the Iravas/Ezhavas (Mal. *īḻavan*), although they were quite rare cases.[39] Undoubtedly, the *marumakkattāyaṃ* system popularized Sanskrit in matrilineal communities as in such families the men educated in Sanskrit language and its literature appeared, arousing the ambition to study it.

In the 19th century the impact of English education started in Kerala. Sanskrit education was slowly replaced by the English model and the Malayalam language was given supremacy over Sanskrit in the case of literature and scholarship. This new type of education proved to be useful in the new political and administrative circumstances and that was the reason why it was gradually beginning to be sought after. Modern, state supported education was more open for people from different backgrounds as well as for women:

> By the 1920s, the first generation of women educated in the modern style was a significant presence in the Malayalee public sphere. Such women were also beginning to gain employment in schools, medical institutions and the government.
> (*Devika 2007: 5*)

[39] This is the caste whose members were Narayana Guru (Skt. *nārāyaṇa guru*; 1854(?)–1928), the Keralan reformer, and Kumaran Asan (Mal. *kumāran āśān*; 1873–1924), the famous Keralan poet as well as philosopher and reformer. They both knew Sanskrit. Kumaran Asan, at a certain time, developed a taste for this language and wrote in it as well as translated Sanskrit literature into Malayalam (George 1968: 148–151).

The tendency to neglect the previous style of education of women started at the end of the 19th century. In one of the novels written at that time, entitled the *Mīn̲ākṣi* by Cheruvalathu Chathu Nair (Mal. *ceṛuvalatu catu nāyar*),[40] the school-based education for women is depicted as an ideal but according to J. Devika also "modernised" Sanskrit education was recommended:

> (...) this does not seem to imply a rejection of all the existent forms of training. For instance, it was something explicitely stated that a Sanskrit-based education which gave importance to *kavyams*, *natakams*, etc. would only promote sensuality, and that by avoiding these and teaching the *Dharmasastras* (moral canon) instead, women could be made virtuous.
> (*Devika 2007: 102–103*)

While analysing the articles published in periodicals, including women's magazines as for instance *Sārabodhini*,[41] it is clearly visible that the proposed pattern of Kerala women education went together with the all-India tendency of how to train girls and build a certain ideal of a modern Indian woman. The main stress was put on a woman's chastity as the direct result of her education. The mythical models of chaste Indian heroines such as Sitā or Savitrī were referred to and reminded to female readers time and again. Queen Victoria also became one of the models, however, the extreme Westernization of women's life was excluded from that pattern. Some authors carefully stressed the fact that a woman should not decide for herself. It is men who are responsible for her life.

There were only very few Malayali women who were recognised as fitting to be the role models for a modern Malayali womenfolk.

---

[40] More about this novel published in 1890 read in: Meenu 2016.

[41] The first women's journal in Kerala, entitled the *Kēralīya Suguṇa Bōdhini*, was established in 1884 in Thiruvananthapuram. The word *bodhinī* (f.) comes from Sanskrit and means "awakening, enlightening". It was used as a part of the titles of the first women's journals; see Dalmia 1999: 245–241.

Among them was Manorama (Mal. *manōrama*, Skt. *manoramā*) Tampuratti, a poetess belonging to a Zamorin's family, whose accomplishments as a Sanskrit scholar will be shown below.

It seems that the middle class Nayar women were the target group of the writers and journalists. Perhaps this class of society was the most open to introducing some changes in their style of life and its womenfolk the most independent.

The Nambudiri girls' access to education was still not easy till almost the middle of the 20th century. Marjatta Parpola describes the inauguration of the school in the Panjal (Mal. *pāññāḷ*) village in 1930. The girls were invited to attend but when the school began, no girls came to study. Parpola also addresses the case of a Nambudiri girl who in 1941 attended the 8th standard outside the village, in fact against the will of her father but supported by other members of her family. Her rite of menstruation was performed secretly but her father got to know about it two months later. The furious father put an end to his daughter's education (Parpola 2000: 190).

4. The daily life of a poetess

We do not know too many details concerning the lives of women writers and scholars of the past. Rājaśekhara, a theoretician of Sanskrit literature living in the 10th CE, in his *Kāvyamīmāṃsā* 10, produces a picture of a day in a poet's life. Also Kṣemendra (10/11th CE), in his *Kavikaṇṭhābharaṇa*, speaks about conditions of a poet's life.[42] It is definitely an idealized picture, although true to a certain degree. He depicts the poet waking up, his daily chores and duties together with the training in his literary profession. Perhaps the idea was inspired by the projection of the day of a king as given in the *Arthaśāstra* or *Manusmṛti*. In the same

[42] See also Lienhard 1984: 13–19.

manner we could sketch the daily life of a Kerala woman from an aristocratic family, with one important difference—this sketch would be, of course, generalization but very close to reality. A brief account of the family environment may give an idea about the female members of such families. The basic culture remains the same, though the ritualistic patterns may show variations in different families. In such orthodox Hindu families the life of a poetess as well as any other female member would be concentrated mainly on religion and family. She, as others, would get up very early in the morning and after her bath in the family pond (a bath under a pipe, or by pouring water will not make one "*śuddha*"—purified—one has to immerse one's self in a pond or river for the purpose) attends to her duties. Only such a person who has purified oneself can attend to the '*pūjā* chores' in the family shrine, prepare food in the kitchen and mingle with other members of the family who have also had their baths. In those days, people who after getting up did not take their baths were considered to be in the *kuliya suddham* (Mal. *kuliya*—unbathed) condition. Similarly, when one went outside and came back home, he or she would be in the *vaḻi suddham* (Mal.*vaḻi*—road, way) condition, namely the condition of those who have been travelling and they can enter the house only after purifying themselves by a bath in a tank along with their clothes. The ladies of the family never touched members of other communities and if by accident or during travel such a thing happened, they would have had to purify themselves by a bath. So after the morning ablution they attended to the arrangements for the morning rituals in the family shrine.

In the Kanjiramattom (Mal. *kāññiramattam*) Palace of Punjar Rajas, the day started for instance with a 'Gaṇapati homam', to propitiate Lord Gaṇeśa. This was followed by *pūjās* to the deities in their shrine.[43] At that time female members, especially, would be in the shrine engaged in *jāpa*, i.e. the repetition of the names

[43] Fieldwork notes taken during my stay in Punjar, February 2015.

of the Lord, or reciting various verses or *ślokas* of hymns praising the deities and praying for their grace and blessings. These will have been over by 8.30 a.m. Then she would go to the kitchen and help with the chores there as well as look after the children. Noon meals were usually around 11.30. After that, it was time for some *purāṇapārāyaṇa*, i.e. studying the texts of *Purāṇas*, recitation of the *Rāmāyaṇa*, *Mahābhārata*, *Bhāgavatam*, etc. Repetition of such religious texts was believed to cultivate the mind to loftier ideals and thoughts. It was also time for reading and writing. Before sunset, there was time for a body wash, leaving the head alone, and again engagement in *jāpa* and recitation of prayers in the family shrine.[44] Female family members in those days lived a cloistered life with very little contact with others.[45] But the habit of reading had exposed them to a lot of information.

Every month, except for *īṭavam* (Mal. Taurus—May/June) and *mithunam* (Mal. Gemini—June/July), had a special religious function, in which the female members of the family had to take part and organize too. The ritual calendar through the months included the following main religious festivals:

ciṅṅam (Mal. Leo, August/September)—in this month there was the Onam (Mal. *ōṇam*), an important festival in Kerala. Now, it has become a state festival too.

---

[44] For information about the ritual life of a Nambudiri woman, i.e. Antarjanam, see: Parpola 2000: 217–230.

[45] A picture of a Nambudiri woman's life one can find in the autobiographies such as *An Introduction to Autobiography* by Lalithambika Antharjanam (1909–1987), a social reformer and writer of prose in Malayalam, and the *Antharjanam* or the *Memoirs of a Namboodiri Woman* by Devaki Nilayamgode. Lalithambika's novel *Fire Being the Witness* (Mal. *Agnisākṣi*) depicts the hardships the women in Nambudiri families had to endure. The novel of Malayalam writer Matampu Kunhukuttan entitled *Bhraṣṭa* (published in 1973 and recently translated into English as the *Outcaste*) shows the revenge of a Nambudiri woman on her community but also depicts the dark side of life of younger brothers in a Nambudiri family. The book is based on a real story that is the famous trial and excommunication of Kuriyedatu Tatri in 1905.

kanni (Mal. Virgo—September/October)—it was time for the *navarātri pūjā*, when the Goddess Sarasvatī is worshipped. The festival lasts for nine days and closes on the tenth day called the *vijayadaśamī*.

tulām (Mal. Libra—October/November)—for the whole month girls perform the Gaṇapati *pūjā* every day.

vṛścikam (Mal. Scorpio—November/December, Skt. Kārttika)—celebration of the birthday of the Goddess.

dhanu (Mal. Sagittarius—December/January)—this is the month when the ladies celebrate a function called *tiruvāttira*,[46] which in the past lasted for one week, now is usually celebrated on one day and the following or preceding night. Its important part is a special group dance called *tiruvāttirakkaḷi* (Mal.). It is performed in the evening to the tunes and lyrics of songs from Kathakali (Mal. *kathakaḷi*) and also those written exclusively for the purpose (Mal. *tiruvāttirappāṭṭŭ*). This celebration is related to the marriage of Lord Śiva with Goddess Pārvatī, when Pārvatī was performing a fast for forty one days.[47] Married women should fast from the day preceding *tiruvāttira* for the wellbeing of their husband and his long life. It is believed that when girls observe *tiruvāttira*, they get good husbands.

makaram (Mal. Capricorn—January/February)—a month special to Lord Ayyappa when male members of the family fast for forty one days with strict celibacy, avoiding non-vegetarian food, alcohol, etc. The house will provide an environment for these fasts.

kumbham (Mal. Aquarius—February/March)—a festival called *śivarātrī* is celebrated, i.e. "the night of Śiva". Again fasting and *pūjās* are involved, and one should not sleep and should remain fully awake all that night.

---

[46] Mal. *tiru*=Skt. *śrī*; Mal. *ātira*=Skt. *ārdrā*=Betelgeuse. The term refers also to the festival days so special for women. More about the festival in Parpola 2000: 224–229.

[47] Another belief connects the festival with Śiva's birthday.

mīnam (Mal. Pisces—March/April)—it is a month devoted to the Goddess and there are special *pūjās* and celebrations, monthly fasts, etc.

mēṭam (Mal. Aries—April/May)—*viṣu puṇyakālam*—originally in Kerala this was the first month of the year. It is an auspicious month and special *pūjās* and gifts to learned Brahmins are given.

karkkaṭakam (Mal. Cancer—July/August)—the month devoted to *pūjās*. There is a special *trikālapūjā*, i.e. the adorations that are done in the morning, midday and evening for twelve days. It is also a month when one undertakes Ayurvedic treatments as a preventive health measure. It is also celebrated as the *Rāmāyaṇamāsam*, when the *Rāmāyaṇa* is recited during the whole month.

Fasts were observed during the *ekādaśī* and *ṣaṣṭhī*, i.e. the 11th and 6th days of a lunar month.

As my respondents highlighted, in olden days, when the present day consumer culture had not made inroads into the families, people lived a life of devotion to God and many religious practices.[48] Chandravali Tampuran stated: "we were taught how to fast, not feast".[49] Definitely, organizing various religious rites and rituals was part and parcel of every woman's life in Kerala. The restrictions due to the caste differences have already been mentioned but as a woman, the poetess had even more limitations and rules to follow. For instance, when women had their menstruation, they themselves were polluted and treated as untouchables. Thus, they could not use some items which they could spoil with their touch. Among such objects, water was one. Homemade ink was prepared with water, that is why touching the ink would have polluted it and the whole liquid would have had to be thrown away. Thus, in such circumstances, a poetess would write her literary works in pencil.[50]

---

[48] From the notes of Dr. R. P. Raja.

[49] Chandravali Tampuran, interview on February 2014.

[50] More about the treatment of menstruating women in the Nambudiri

At the turn of the nineteenth and twentieth centuries writing material changed from cadjan leaves to paper. But then, paper or notebooks were not so easily available, one had to write on whatever piece of paper came one's way. Our imagined poetess would be in the same situation.

The question connected with the circulation of women's poems and other works, and consequently their audience, is intriguing but in this respect no pattern can be given. The distribution and preservation of a literary oeuvre differed in the case of different poetesses as we will be able to see later on. As was mentioned above, in the nineteenth century several women's journals were edited in India, also in Kerala. It seems—these journals were an ideal place for our imagined Keralan poetess to publish her works. Kerala was also not deprived of printing houses. To the contrary, the first "extant printed matter produced in India in an Indian language using an Indian script" (Galewicz 2019: 105) comes from the printing press in Quilon (Mal. *kollaṃ*)[51] on the Malabar coast. There were many printing houses in Kerala and some of them, perhaps nineteenth-century ones, still exist and are in use, producing leaflets and different booklets exactly as the Narendra Printers at Mannadiar Lane (Fig. 6, p. 84) in Trichur (Mal. *tṛśūr*) I visited in 2005 does. In such places women writers could also print their works, provided there was funding for that. After drawing these hypothetical pictures from the life of a Malayali woman writer, let us use the words of Tara Puri as a kind of conclusion:

> From the 1970s, feminist scholars have been turning to the archive to look for texts by women, texts that would challenge the literary

and Nayar communities, especially the rite of the first menstruation (Mal. *tiraṇṭukalyāṇaṃ*) see in Parpola 2000: 181–189.

[51] "Otherwise known as the "small catechism," this *Doutrina Christã* had been published in A.D. 1578 by a press run by Jesuits at the Collegio do Saluador in a Portuguese fort built in the coastal town of Kollam" (Galewicz 2019: 105).

canon and reshape linear and discrete understandings of national histories. Despite this ongoing scholarly work, rejuvenated by a more recent 'archival turn' in historical studies, women's writings, the archives of women's organisations, and the ordinary artefacts of women's lives (letters, photographs, material possessions) remain understudied (...).
(*Puri 2018: 47*)

II. Women's Writing in Travancore

1. Introduction. Sanskrit literature and scholarship in Kerala—its past and present

It is difficult to say exactly when Sanskrit culture settled for good in Kerala, but it may be assumed that its influence in the seventh century CE was already significant.[52] Daṇḍin, a theoretician of Sanskrit literature and writer, at all probability active between 680 and 720 CE (Bronner 2012: 76), in the autobiographical part of *Avantisundarīkathā*, mentions his friends from Kerala who are great scholars and teachers and the authors of commentaries on the Vedic *kalpasūtras*, that is, texts related to rituals and sacrifices.[53] For sure then, both the Vedic religion and Brahmins who promoted it were well-established in Kerala. The migration of Brahmins to this area of Southern India, absorbing the customs of both the previous arrivals and autochthons as well as adding new habits, also those dictated by life in a new environment, caused a very

[52] Moser and Younger write: "Many of these settlements were given to Brahmans by members of the Cera dynasty when it briefly revived near Muziris between the ninth and thirteenth centuries, but weaker rulers had certainly started the practice earlier and Brahman landholdings continued to accumulate in the centuries that followed" (Moser and Younger 2013: 140).

[53] From the *Avantisundarī* we learn that some great Vedic scholars such as Mātṛdatta and Devaśarman arrived from Kerala to meet Daṇḍin (... *bhūmidevanivahacūḍāmaṇir devaśarmā tvaddarśanāya keralebhyaḥ*) (Daṇḍin, *Avantisundarī*, ed. Śūranāḍ Kuñjan Pilla,1954: 14).

specific group of Brahmins called the Nambudiris to appear in Kerala.[54] This particular community, as we already know, was responsible for preserving Sanskrit culture, continuing Sanskrit studies, maintaining institutions where Vedic texts and *śāstras*, scientific disciplines helping to understand and preserve the Vedas were studied. There was a time when maintaining science and schools at an appropriate level had, above all, a very specific goal: well-prepared scholars could overcome the debates of Buddhists and Jainas, who had had their supporters in the South of India for a long time. There were monastic and educational centres established for deepening of Vedic studies (Mal. *maṭham*), some of which specialized in the *śāstras*. There were also academies associated with temples (Skt. *śālā*) (Galewicz 2015: 73–74). From at least the 7th century till the end of the 19th century, there was a continuous growth in all branches of Sanskrit learning including the creation of belles lettres. To that picture one has to add Vedic rituals carefully preserved by the Nambudiri Brahmins up to the present day (e.g. Galewicz 2002, 2003, 2004; Staal 1961; Staal 1983).

These facts only help us to realize the importance of Sanskrit culture in Kerala and its long history up to modern times. The new patterns of education introduced in Kerala in the 19th century reduced the importance of Sanskrit studies. However, there were still centres of Sanskrit learning encouraged by local royal families. The Kodungallur Royal Family created a very important ambience for intellectuals consisting of famous Sanskrit scholars. Among them were also the members of the royal family themselves, for instance Kodungallur Kocchunni Tampuran (Mal. *koccuṇṇi*), who was given the title 'Kavisarvabhouman' (Skt. *kavisārvabhauma*, i.e. an emperor of the poets) (Subramanian 2008: 14–15). Even now there are Keralites who write in Sanskrit employing traditional genres (e.g. a modern *mahākāvya* entitled *Keralodaya* authored

[54] More about Brahmins of Kerala in Parpola 2000 and Galewicz 2015.

by K. N. Ezhuttacchan, published in 1977) but also experimenting with new forms and new media of transmission, e.g. a musical radio play *Santānagopāla* by Ambadi Devaki Amma (Kunjunni Raja 1958: 274). There are also Sanskrit translations or adaptations of famous works written in Malayalam or other languages (e.g. the *Uddālakacarita*, a prose version of Shakespeare's *Othello* by A. R. Rajaraja Varma [Raghavan 1964: 110]; the poem *Nalinī* of Kumaran Asan, a famous Malayalam poet, translated into Sanskrit; the Tamil epic *Cilappatikāram* rendered into a Sanskrit poem of six cantos by C. Narayan Nair [Kunjunni Raja 1980: 273]).

Kunjunni Raja's *Contribution of Kerala to Sanskrit literature* is a good source to become acquainted with the vast in bulk and varied in contents literary output of Kerala. There are also works in Malayalam which guide those familiar with the Malayalam language through this real ocean of literature, for instance the *Kēraḷīyasaṃskṛtasāhityacaritṟaṃ* by Vadakkumkur Rajaraja Varma Raja (Mal. *vaṭakkuṃkūr rājarājavarma rāja*) or parts of Ullur S. Parameswara Iyer's (Mal. *uḷḷūr paramēśvarayyar*) *Kēraḷasāhityacaritraṃ*. There are other useful tools for researchers in Kerala Sanskrit literature, namely bibliographies prepared by E. Easwaran Nampoothiry (published in 1972) and a more detailed one, published in 1997 by S. Venkitasubramonia Iyer.

Even a brief survey into the subject gives a picture of astonishing richness. The researchers from abroad are conscious of the presence of some works although little has been done to bring them to the attention of international scholarship. The so-called Trivandrum Manuscript containing the plays attributed to Bhāsa[55] directed scholarly interests towards performing arts of Kerala, such as *kūṭiyāṭṭam* and *kathakaḷi*.[56] There are also researchers in Ker-

[55] The question of their authorship has been the subject of scholarly debate among Sanskrit scholars, see for instance Tieken 1993 and 1997, Bhāsa Project of Heidrun Brückner.

[56] See the *kūṭiyāṭṭam* bibliography by Heike Moser (Oberlin):

ala who deal with Sanskrit literary heritage of their homeland. These are N. V. P. Unnithiri, Narayanan Parameswaran Unni, Venu Gopalan, C. Rajendran, Karakkattil Gheevarghese Paulose and many others. Thanks to some of them many texts have been edited and are accessible to the Indological world. Nevertheless, still a lot of work has to be done.

2. The Travancore Royal House and its intellectual environment

In addition to different centres of Sanskrit learning in Kerala, such as temple *maṭhas*, *śālās* and schools in traditional *gurukula* system, the courts of kings were an important place to promote Sanskrit writings. It is not only about the royal patronage but a great number of these kings were scholars and poets themselves. And such a development was characteristic of many royal families, whereas the establishing of the real royal *sabhās*, i.e. the gatherings of scholars and litterati, was possible for powerful rulers only and lasted as long as their lifetime. The courts of the rulers were the ambience in which one could expect the presence of women literati too. Let us start with Travancore.

It is not my intention to go into a detailed discussion devoted to the history of Travancore. Suffice to mention a few historical facts.

The word Travancore, being an Anglicized form of Tiruvitāṅkūr, may come from the *honorificum tiruvaṭi* used by the Venad (Mal. *vēnāṭu*˘) rulers (Vielle 2012: 366) or directly from the name of the site Tiruvitamcode, "the seat of the southern branch of the Vēṇāḍu family (...) located in the region, but its palace is now

https://publikationen.uni-tuebingen.de/xmlui/handle/10900/46921 and also the project *Kudiyattam: Living Sanskrit Theater in the Kerala* (http://kudiyattam.huji.ac.il).

gone" (Heston 1996: 83). In the Chera period Venad developed into a big and powerful region. At that time different *svarūpams*[57] ruled over smaller or bigger parts of it, functioning as "lineage segments, with bonds of kinship existing among them, but acting as independent chiefs in their respective areas" (Ganesh 2002: 224). The members of the ruling houses were placed in different residences, i.e. *kōyikkal*s (Mal.), accordingly to their seniority and rights. In the course of time such a *kōyikkal* was established also in Tiruvitamcode. In this political mosaic of medieval Venad there were also maternal ancestral houses (Mal. *tāyavali*) connected with certain lineages. The Attingal (Mal. *āttiṅgal*)[58] 'motherhouse' played a crucial role here. The most important economicwise were two localities: Kollam (Mal. *kollaṃ/koḷaṁbam*; Anglicized as Quilon), an international port of trade, and Nanchilnad (Mal. *nāñcilnāṭu˘*), the largest paddy region. So no wonder that, in the words of K. N. Ganesh:

> Dēśiṅganāṭu which benefited by the trade in Kollam and Trippāppūr, which mobilised the resources in Nāñcilnāṭu and had the backing of the Padmanābha temple, emerged as the mayor players. (*Ganesh 2002: 165*)

Desinganad (Mal. *dēśiṅganāṭu˘*) is also called Kallada (Mal. *kallaḍa*) Svarupam. Trippapur (Mal. *tṛppāppūr*) was the name of a residence (near Tiruvanantapuram), from which the seat was moved to a palace at Tiruvitamcodu (Sreedhara Menon 2006: 199). Till the 14th century members of the ruling family of this area were

---

[57] The term *svarūpam* is used in two meanings—a royal lineage and a territory controlled by such a family, a pre-state formation as some scholars call it "with various components of a state such as massive body of bureaucratic functionaries, subordinate *sthānams*, local magnates, a treasury, mint, and an army which was ready to act as and when needed though not in the form of a standing military form" (Champakalakshmi et al 2002: 33). See also Ganesh 2014: 46–48.

[58] Attingal figures in different Sanskrit sources as the Kūpaka country. More about Attingal queens in J. Nair & K. S. Nair 2001.

in fact identified with one more residence, namely Kilperur (Mal. *kīḻpērūr*). Sometimes the combined form Kilperur-Trippapur appears in the records. From the 14th century onwards only Trippapur Svarupam was mentioned. Padmanabha Menon in his *History of Kerala Written in the Form of Notes on Visscher's Letters from Malabar* informs that "the house name of Kīḻpērūr" was also added to the personal designations of the Rajas of "Cheravāi, and Ḍēśingaṇād branches" (Padmanabha Menon 1993: 8). There is not enough evidence to understand the situation fully but there are continuous attempts to explain the processes leading to changes in early-modern socio-political structures of the region (e.g. Devadevan 2014; Ganesh 2014; Narayanan 2013; Veluthat 2013; Vielle 2012; Vielle 2014).

The practice of mutual adoptions[59] among the Desinganad, Trippappur, Kottarakara (Mal. *koṭṭārakkara*) and Attingal families at the beginning of the 17th century added a lot to establishing the seniority order in Venad. The territories of Trippappur Svarupam expanded absorbing the areas of the tiny kingdoms of Tekkumkur (Mal. *tekkūṃkūr*), Vadakkumkur, Kayamkulam (Mal. *kāyaṃkulaṃ*) and other ones to constitute finally the kingdom of Travancore. In this way the patchwork quilt of this region become more homogeneous and this process of unification continued until the mid-18th century. During the reign of king Martanda Varma (1729–1758) the state attained almost its final territorial configuration and modern structure due to reforms and reorganisation implemented by its ruler. *Mahārāja* changed the old name of the capital from Kalkulam to Padmanabhapuram (Skt. *padmanābhapura*) (Figs 7–8, p. 84) in 1744 (Heston 1996: 83). The Hindu character of the state was underlined by the spectacular act of its ruler: in 1750 Martanda Varma dedicated the kingdom to his tutelary deity Sri Padmanabha (Skt. *śrīpadmanābha*) and ruled as his servant—*dāsa* (Skt.). From that time the rulers of Travancore

[59] About the practice of adoption in Malabar, see Wigram 1882: 4–5.

adopted this title, which meant that they ruled in the name of this particular god. It was an important move to legitimize a newly created state and underline that its rulers maintained and protected the Hindu *dharma* in their domain and Travancore became known as *dharmabhūmi*—the land on which the law and Hindu religion was observed. Martanda Varma is considered the founder of modern Travancore (Shreedhara Menon 2006: 293; Ibrahimkunju 2007: 182; Nagam Aiya 1906: 182). His successor was his nephew Balarama Varma (Skt., Mal. *bālarāmavarma*), born in 1724 under the *kārttika* (Mal. < Skt. *kṛttikā*[60]) asterism, and hence known as Karttika Tirunal Rama Varma. He was also called Dharmaraja (reign 1758–1798). He moved his seat from Padmanabhapuram to Tiruvanantapuram. Avittam[61] Tirunal Balarama Varma (1798–1810) was the next *mahārāja*. After his reign, on 16 November 1810, Rani Lakshmi Bayi (Mal. *rāṇi*[62] *lakṣmi bāyi*) ascended the throne and ruled till 1815. Then the regency of Gauri Parvati Bayi (Mal. *gauri pārvati bāyi*) lasted till 1829. Her son Svati[63] Tirunal Rama Varma was born in 1813 and died in 1847 at the age of 34. The line of the kings of Travancore has continued and still exists. The last actual ruler of Travancore was Śri Chithira[64] Tirunal Balarama Varma (r. 1931–1949) (Shreedhara Menon 2006: 170). There are many sources describing and analysing different aspects of their rule, also the contacts with Europeans who made their appearance in Kerala, however, we are going to concentrate on the 18th- and 19th-century royal courts as centres promoting Sanskrit culture. Among the sources to the history of Travancore, as well as other south Indian kingdoms, one can find correspondence

[60] The third lunar mansion.

[61] Mal. *aviṭṭam*, Skt. *śraviṣṭha*—the 23rd asterism (Delphinus).

[62] Mal. *rāṇi* < Pkt. *rāṇī* < Skt. *rājñī*—queen; title of Venad queens.

[63] Skt. *svāti*, the name of the star Arcturus, forming the 13th or, according to modern reckoning, 15th lunar asterism.

[64] Mal. *cittira*, Skt. *citrā*—the fourteenth lunar mansion.

and accounts of travellers, the officials of East India Company, as for instance the rapport of Francis Buchanan (1807) in three volumes,[65] a meticulous work in two volumes entitled *Malabar* by William Logan, the Collector of the District and the works of missionaries, such as Hermann Gundert. But from the second half of the 19th century the publication of the first modern histories of Travancore written by Southerners starts. As Udaya Kumar writes:

> Vaikkathu Pachu Moothathu [Vaykattu Pāccu Mūttatu] published his *Tiruvitaṅkūr Caṟitram* (A History of Travancore) in 1867. Sir T. Madhava Rao also attempted a history of Travancore, but confined himself to a period of seventy years in the eighteen century. K. Shangoonny Menon's more elaborate *History of Travancore*, written in English, was published in 1878. All three were royalist histories, which organised their material under the periods of reign of various sovereigns of Travancore. Pachu Moothathu was a scholar of Sanskrit, a grammarian, an astrologer, and a renowned medical practitioner. Although he was concerned to establish the accuracy of his narrative by referring to primary sources, his motives in writing a history of Travancore were primarily ethical and pedagogical (...)
> (*Kumar 2010: 24*)

The historians active in the twentieth and twenty-first centuries consider a wide range of different sources in order to reconstruct the history of Kerala, analysing also the history of Travancore. The edition of literary texts has brought new pieces of information too.

---

[65] *Journey from Madras through the Countries of Mysore, Canara, and Malabar Performed under the Order of the Most Noble Marquis Wellesley, Governor General of India for the Express Purpose of Investigation the State of Agriculture, Arts, and Commerce; the Religion, Manners, and Customs; the History Natural and Civil, and Antiquities, in the Dominions of the Rajah of Mysore, and the Countries Acquired by the Honourable East India Company, in the Late and Former Wars, from Tippoo Sultaun*, London 1807.

There are also publications of the members of royal families. Princess Aswathi Thirunal Gouri Lakshmi Bayi has published a monograph on Sri Padmanabha Temple in Trivandrum in the year 2000. The biography *At the Turn of the Tide: the Life and Times of Maharani Setu Lakshmi Bayi, the Last Queen of Travancore* was written by her granddaughter Dr. Lakshmi Raghunandan and published in 1995, on the 100th anniversary of Maharani's birth.[66] Dr. R. P. Raja, wrote the monograph *New Light on Swathi Thirunal.* The access to the royal family archives was also given to the journalist Uma Maheswari, who in 2015 edited the volume *Sree Chithira Tirunal Life and Times.*

From 1729, the year in which Martanda Varma began his reign, till 1949—the last year of Chithira Tirunal Balarama Varma's rule, that is for a period of 220 years, there were twelve sovereigns who ruled Travancore. Among them were also women, although just one of them, Ayiliyam[67] Tirunal Gauri Lakshmi Bayi, was a real sovereign, the others being regents only. They all contributed to the development of the state, took care of education and patronized artists and poets. What is more, some of them were also writers and composers.

2.1. At the court of Dharmaraja

King Martanda Varma, mentioned as the maker of modern Travancore, was a patron of many scholars and poets. Among important personages supported by him, it is enough to mention Ramapanivada (*rāmapāṇivāda*), a prolific writer, who authored dramas, epic poems, shorter poems[68] as well as works on grammar, prosody,

[66] Also Manu S. Pillai (Pillai 2015) concentrates mainly on the life of Setu Lakshmi Bayi in his *The Ivory Throne: Chronicles of the House of Travancore.*

[67] Mal. *āyiliyam* < Skt. āśleṣa, the 9th asterism.

[68] E.g. *Śārikāsandeśa*, a messenger poem edited with a Sanskrit commentary and a critical study by C. M. Nilakandhan. The editor provides also

dance and music. Another poet, Devaraja (Skt. *devarāja*), migrated to Travancore from Tamilnadu, and was well received at the court. His drama *Bālamārtāṇḍavijayam*[69] commemorates the dedication of the kingdom to Śri Padmanābha and other important events of the King's rule. Martanda Varma's successor, Rama Varma (reign 1758–98), did even more to promote literature and learning. Karttika Tirunal Rama Varma was born in 1724 as a son of Kerala Varma Koyil Tampuran of Kilimanur and Rani Parvati Bayi. King Martanda Varma, whose successor was Karttika Tirunal Rama Varma, was his maternal uncle. The education of this young prince was very thorough and he proved to be a very talented pupil who mastered several languages: Sanskrit, Persian, Hindustani, English and Portuguese. He had also some knowledge of Dutch. He was gifted not only at languages but also for arts (Sāmbaśiva Śāstrī 1935: 4). He wrote the *Bālarāmabharata*, a treatise based on the *Nāṭyaśāstra*, and several Kathakali plays. He was a patron to different scholars and poets.[70] As Fra Bartolomeo mentioned, the processions of the *mahārāja* were accompanied not only by a band of musicians, but also by "two court-poets who celebrated in songs his great achievements" (Sāmbaśiva Śāstrī 1935: 14). Among his court poets was his friend Devaraja, who started his career under king Martanda Varma[71] and was given the title of New Kalidasa (Skt. *navakālidāsa*) by him. A great number of eminent literati gathered at his court writing mainly in Sanskrit

information about Ramapanivada and names all his works.

[69] The drama was edited by K. Sāmbhaśiva Sāstri in 1930.

[70] More about his role as a scholar and patron in the article: "*Bālarāmabharata* of Kartika Tirunal Balarama Varma: the patronage of the Rajahs of Travancore" by Agnieszka Wójcik (forthcoming).

[71] According to the *Diaries* of Ananda Ranga Pillai, a famous *dubash* of the French East India Company, Martanda Varma sent his poet on a mission to Governor-General of French India, Joseph F. Dupleix, in 1747 (Sāmbaśiva Śāstrī 1935: 15). About the results of this assignment read in Kusuman 1987: 95.

but also in Malayalam, as for instance Kunjan Nambiar (Mal. *kuñcan nampiyār*).[72] During his reign Kerala was invaded by Hyder Ali (c. 1720–1782) and his son and successor Tipu Sultan of Mysore. Many people sought shelter in Travancore as it was the only part of Kerala which remained outside the Mysorean authority. In 1789–1790 Tipu Sultan attempted to defeat Travancore but the King with his army took the fight, and so did the East India Company's army (Travancore became a British ally state), and finally Tipu retreated to his capital. Rama Varma came to be known as Dharmaraja (Skt. *dharmarājan*), a protector against foreign invasion. Among the refugees there were also talented poets. Dharmaraja, a poet and scholar himself, did not refuse his protection to anyone. In his *Bālarāmabharata* he says:

> *kalibhayacakitā ye deśadeśaprasiddhā nṛpabhayacakitā*
> *ye sādhavaḥ sādhuvṛttāḥ /*
> *aśaraṇam iti matvā deśato gantukāmāḥ śaraṇam*
> *upagatās te vañcibhūpāladeśam //35//*[73]

> These virtuous sages, famous in different countries,
> who were trembling with fear of clash,
> quaking in terror of the [invading] king,
> they, conscious of having no protection
> and wishing to leave their country,
> went seeking shelter to the ruler of the kingdom of Vañci[74] [75]

One of such refugees was a certain Nambudiri from Malabar (Sāmbaśiva Śāstrī 1935: 13). The messenger poem (Skt. *sandeśakāvya, dūtakāvya*) entitled *Cātakasandeśa* composed by him is quite unusual, as it is a supplication for some maintenance directed to King

---

[72] More in Kunjunni Raja 1980: 168–180.

[73] *Bālarāmabharatam of Śrī Bālarāma Varma Vanci Maharaja*. K. Sāmbaśiva Śāstrī (ed.), 1935: 6.

[74] The title *vañcirāja* or *vañcibhūpa* refers to the supposed connections of the rulers of Travancore and the Cheras.

[75] All translations from Sanskrit are mine unless otherwise stated.

Rama Varma.[76] As an aftermath of Tipu's invasion the author lost everything, that is why he begs the King in the same way as *cātaka* birds[77] ask the cloud for drops of water. Among the refugees seeking protection at the court of Travancore, there was also one more person we have to mention here—Manorama Tampuratti. For us this guest of Dharmaraja is of utmost importance. It goes without saying that besides men with scholarly and literary achievements to their credit, there were also talented and educated women, who could contribute a lot to different fields of learning and poetry, provided their contribution would be circulated and made known.

2.2. Manorama Tampuratti—a royal guest of Dharmaraja

Manorama Tampuratti belonged to the royal family of the Zamorins who ruled from Calicut. They were descendants of the Chera governors of Eranad or Eralanad (Mal. *ēranāṭu˘/ēraḷanāṭu˘*), so they were the Samanta section of the Nayars (Krishna Ayyar 1938: 1).[78] Nediyiruppu (Mal. *neṭiyiruppu*), a hilly region near Maḻappuram (Mal. *malappuṟam*), is believed to be their ancestral place, hence the royal family is known as the Nediyiruppu Svarupam. E. K. Govinda Varma Raja, the biographer of the late Eralpad[79] P. K. S. Raja (b. 22.03.1913; d. 27.09.2013), explains that:

[76] One more messenger poem expressing a poet's supplication to his patron is the *Vāgmaṇḍanaguṇadūtakāvya.* To this poem a Ph.D. thesis of Lidia Szczepanik was devoted: *Come Fly with Me. Messengers in Indian Skies. A study of Sanskrit dūtakāvya poetry with reference to the Vāgmaṇḍanaguṇadūtakāvya of Vireśvara* (Jagiellonian University, Kraków, 2015, unpublished).

[77] Skt. *cātaka*—*Clamator jacobinus.* A bird according to Indian believes drinks only from the clouds, and, therefore, it is eagerly expectant of rains.

[78] Other traditions concerning the origin of the Zamorins are given in the *Mediaeval Kerala* by P. K. S. Raja in the chapter "The Ascendency of the Zamorins", pp. 20–31.

[79] Mal. *erālpāṭu˘*—the title of a crown prince in the Zamorin family.

> Originally, Zamorins family was one unit. The Thampuratties used to stay in a palace called Ambadi Kovilakam west of Thali temple in its immediate vicinity. But after adoption of the sisters from Nileswaram Kovilakam, the family split into three. The eldest sister of Kizhekke Kovilakam stayed in the palace in Chinthavalappu, North of the present Zamorin's High School. There is no trace of the palace now. The next younger sister stayed in a palace named Puthiya Kovilakam west of the Thali Tank. Even in 1930, the ruins of this Palace, its ancient gateway and the steps leading into the Thali Tank were there.
> (*Govinda Varma Raja 2007: 16*)

Manorama was born in 1760 as a member of the Kilakke Kovilakam (Mal. *ki<u>l</u>akke kōvilakam*[80]). We do not know if she wrote any particular work in Sanskrit but her reputation as an eminent Sanskrit scholar has survived her. The names of her teachers are known[81] and at least one of her pupils achieved fame. This is Arur Madhavan Atitiri (Mal. *ārūrmādhavan aṭitiri*), the author of the *Uttaranaiṣadha*, in which he praises his teacher:

> *yaṃ vidyārthinam arthapoṣam*
> *apuṣad rājñī puromandira-*
> *kṣmābhṛtsandhupavaṃśabhūḥ*
> *suviduṣī vidyutprakāśā bhuvi* //[82]
>
> This highly learned queen, belonging to the race
> of the Kings of Ocean, resembling the lightening on earth,
> was feeding this pupil with nourishing wealth/meanings.

Sambasiva Sastri in his *Introduction* to the edition of King Karttika Tirunal Balarama Varma's *Bālarāmabharata* writes that in his opinion: "(...) great as the culture of women is in Kerala, no

[80] Mal. *kōvilakam*—royal residence, especially in Malabar.

[81] One of them was Rudra Variyar of the Deśamangalam family. The members of this family were the preceptors of the Zamorins starting from the 15th c. CE (Martin-Dubost 1983: 131).

[82] The Sanskrit text after Kunjunni Raja 1980: 115.

lady has risen to her level of Sanskrit scholarship either before or after" (Sāmbaśiva Śāstrī 1935: 14).

Tradition has it that as a twelve-year-old girl she was able to recite and explain Bhaṭṭoji Dīkṣita's *Prauḍhamanoramā*, an autocommentary to his grammatical treatise *Siddhāntakaumudī*. That is why she was called Manorama.

After the death of her first husband, Rama Varma of the Beypur (Anglicized Beypore; Mal. *beypūr*) royal family, she became the wife of Pākkaṭṭu Bhaṭṭatiri (Martin-Dubost 1983: 132). Alas, he did not know the grammar of Sanskrit at all![83] Manorama expressed her sheer disappointment composing a stanza known up till now to Sanskrit scholars in Kerala:

> *yasya ṣaṣṭhī caturthī ca vihasya ca vihāya /*
> *ahaṃ kathaṃ dvitīyā syād dvitīyā syām ahaṃ kathaṃ //*[84]

> For him, who thinks that *vihasya* and *vihāya* are the sixth
> and the fourth cases and *aham* is the second case,
> how can I be the second (i.e. the better-half, a wife)?

The sixth (Skt. *ṣaṣṭhī*) is a genitive case and the *-sya* would be an ending of masculine and neuter nouns of the a-stem declension, whereas *vihāya* could be mistaken by someone with a very basic knowledge of Sanskrit grammar for the dative, i.e. the fourth case

[83] The situation reminds that one which finally resulted in composing the *Kathāsaritsāgara*: the King did not know Sanskrit and while his learned Queen asked him to stop splashing water on her saying in Sanskrit "modakam" (i.e. *mā*—a particle of prohibition plus *udaka*—water), he ordered sweets for her, that is *modakam*. In this way the King displayed his poor knowledge of Sanskrit. Another uneducated husband, according to legend, was Kālidāsa, who only through the grace of Goddess acquired the knowledge which enabled him the creation of his masterpieces. In the case of Manorama's husband, we do not know if he had taken any steps to gain a better knowledge of Sanskrit as did the partners of both highly educated royal ladies.

[84] Kunjunni Raja 1980: 115.

and *aham* for the second, i.e. accusative case. Now, it is easy to imagine the disappointment of someone who had been able to discuss complex grammar topics since childhood.

Interestingly enough, the same stanza was used by V. Raghavan, a Sanskrit scholar as well as a poet, playwright and musicologist, who composed three one-act plays in Sanskrit devoted to three Sanskrit poetesses of the past: Vijayāṅkā (Skt.; 7th–9th c. CE?), Vikaṭanitambā (Skt.; 9th c. CE?) and Avantisundarī (Skt.; 10th c. CE). Vikaṭanitambā's verses are preserved in anthologies and in works of theoreticians of Sanskrit literature. According to Bhoja (11th c. CE) and Namisādhu (Skt.; 11th c. CE), a commentator on Rudraṭa's (Skt.) *Kāvyālaṅkāra*, her husband could not even pronounce Sanskrit words properly, omitting or mispronouncing the sibilant *ṣa* or the semivowel *ra* in the word *uṣṭra*. Instead of *māsa* (month) he used to say *māṣa* (beans), whereas asked about grain, he declared it to be a month.[85] This verse appears in chapter 31 of Bhoja's treatise entitled *Śṛṅgāraprakāśa*.[86] The chapter treats about sending a messenger and illustrates a case when the heroine's (*nāyikā*) female friend informs her about her suitor (*Śṛṅgāraprakāśa*, ed. Saini 2001: 2037). However, V. Raghavan, describing the scene, adds the verse quoted above, traditionally connected with Manorama.[87]

At the court of Karttika Tirunal Maharaja (Fig. 9, p. 85), Manorama was treated as a guest and perhaps a partner in scholarly discussions. There were suggestions that Manorama helped the King in composing his *magnum opus*, *Bālarāmabharata*, and

---

[85] It seems that the motif of a wife better educated in Sanskrit than her husband is recurrent in Indian narrative tradition.

[86]

pṛṣṭaḥ kale vadati samāṣaṃ tad viparītaṃ sasyam araṇye /
lumpati coṣṭre raṃ vā ṣaṃ vā tasmai dattā vikaṭanitambā //132//

[87] I owe the information about the presence of that stanza in Raghavan's play to Marta Karcz, a Ph.D. candidate at the University of Cagliari, who carries out research on modern Sanskrit literature.

that Dharmaraja was in love with her. They were exchanging letters with verses of mutual admiration. Kunjunni Raja gives examples of such stanzas according to the tradition exchanged by the couple[88]:

> *King:*
> *hemāmbhojini rājahaṃsanivahair āsvādyamānāsave*
> *bhṛṅgo 'ham navamañjarikṛtapadas tvām eva kiñcid bruve /*
> *ceto me bhavadīyapuṣpamakarandāsvādane saspṛham*
> *vācyavācyavicāramārgavimukho lokeṣu kāmī janaḥ //*
>
> Oh, you, possessing golden lotuses!
> Oh, you, who are nectar enjoyed by many geese!
> I, who am a bee, taking [your] feet for fresh flower buds,
> will tell you something:
> My mind is desirous to taste the juice of your flower.
> On this earth people in love are lacking ways to judge
> what should be said and what should not.
>
> *Manorama:*
> *dhīman sadguṇavāridhe tava manovṛttir mahākovidair*
> *durjñeyā svata eva lolahṛdayair nārījanaiḥ kiṃ punaḥ /*
> *tvatsandeśam idam kim artham iti no niścinmahe krīḍitum*
> *kiṃ vā sāmpratam asmadīyahṛdayajñānāya hāsāya vā //*
>
> Oh, learned one! Oh, you, the ocean of excellent qualities!
> The disposition of your mind, by its nature, is difficult
> to understand by great experts, let alone reckless women.
> What is the meaning of your message? I cannot decide now:
> to have fun or to know my mind or to mock?

Manorama Tampuratti left Travancore when the war was over. She died in 1828 (Kunjunni Raja 1980: 115).

As was stated previously, usually we know very little about the lives of women writers or scholars. Here we receive quite a vivid picture, showing an educated, independent and bold woman, although as the only literary legacy a handful of orally transmitted

[88] Kunjunni Raja 1980: 116. The translation is mine.

stanzas ascribed to her have been preserved. It is worth considering the reasons why her actions have become memorable and she has managed to secure a place for herself in Keralites' memory and found the way to the literary histories written in Malayalam as well as in the English language and some of the stanzas of Manorama have been translated also into French.[89] Most probably one of the reasons for her historical visibility was connected with the invasion of Hyder Ali and his son and successor Tipu Sultan of Mysore.[90] In such a way, due to her direct involvement in memorable events, Manorama herself could become more visible and her own reputation as a Sanskrit scholar could flourish on the two courts, where she could also participate in public life. Such a guest could add to the splendour of Karttika Tirunal Balarama Varma's court and help in building the image of him as Dharmaraja. Perhaps the stay at the Travancorean court, at that time a powerful political and cultural centre, helped a lot, even if it was one of the factors in providing her the access to the sphere of the memorable.

2.3. Poetesses of the Travancore Royal Family

Among the royal blood women writers, the name of Princess Ayiliyam Tirunal Rukmini Bayi (Mal. *rukmiṇi bāyi*), the daugther of Rani Gouri Lakshmi Bayi and Raja Raja Varma Koyil Tampuran of the Lakshmi Palace, Changanacherry, should be mentioned. She was born on 28th February 1809. She received a very thorough and broad education together with her two younger brothers, a well known composer Svati Tirunal Rama Varma (born 16th April

[89] I owe the information about the French translation of verses ascribed to Manorama and present in Martin-Dubost's *Poéms D'Amour du Kerala* to Christophe Vielle.

[90] More about Mysorean attack on Malabar in: Ibrahimkunju 2007: 213–234, Ibrahimkunju 1975, Sreedhara Menon 2006: 306–317.

1813, died 1846)[91] and Utram[92] Tirunal Martanda Varma (born 17th August 1814, died 1860). P. Shungoonny Menon (1815–1879), a subordinate officer of the king from 1835 to 1846 and a close associate of both Svati Tirunal and his younger brother, writes:

> The worthy guardian of the royal children took great pains in the management and education of the Princess Rugmini Bhye, who now attained her tenth year, had become a tolerably good scholar in Sanscrit, had studied many works of ancient authors and composed slokams in Sanscrit: she was also well trained in native music, and could play on everall kinds of musical instruments, such as veenah, surunggee (guitar), tamburine, etc.
> (*Shungoonny 1985: 389*)

We are not able to trace her Sanskrit poems but a few of her musical compositions have been preserved and are the subject of research of R. P. Raja, the author of a book "New Light on Swathi Thirunal".[93] Among the women of the Travancore Royal Family one comes across the name of Bharani[94] Tirunal Rani Lakshmi Bayi, another poet and composer among the members of the Royal Family of Travancore. Born in 1848, in the branch of the Kolattunad (Mal. *kōlattunāṭu*˘[95]) Royal Family, she was adopted by the Travancore house in 1857, when the niece of Utram Tirunal Martanda Varma, Rani Puradam[96] Lakshmi Bayi, died soon after

[91] Svati Tirunal, although very much interested in promoting literature and poets, musicians and their compositions as well as dancers (Raja 2006: 209–214), contributed also to the welfare of the state and people. He established free English schools in the state, the dispensaries, the first hospital under government administration, the first government press. The Trivandrum Public Library owes its origin to his patronage (Raja 2006: 205–209).

[92] Skt. *uttara*, Mal. *utraṃ/uttiraṃ*—12th asterism, the tail of Leo.

[93] Personal communication 30.1.2015.

[94] Skt. *bharaṇi/bharaṇī*—the 7th asterism.

[95] The kingdom of the Kolattiri (Mal. *kōlattiri*) dynasty of North Malabar related to the royal house of Travancore.

[96] Mal. *pūrādaṃ* < Skt. *pūrvāṣāḍhā*, the 18th or 20th lunar asterism.

giving birth to a son. In the matrilineal family the lack of continuators of the female line would threaten the existence of the dynasty as it was a son of the king's niece who could be a ruler. Thus, as in the previous such incidents, it was decided to adopt two girls from the Kolattunad family, this time from its branch settled in the Mavelikkara Tekke Kottaram (Mal. *māvēlikkaṟa tekke koṭṭāraṃ*[97]). Bharani Tirunal Lakshmi Bayi became the Senior Rani and in 1858 she married Kerala Varma Koyil Tampuran of the Lakshmipuram Palace, who later on was known as Kālidāsa of Kerala. P. K. Narayana Pillai, who wrote Kerala Varma's biography and translated his Malayalam poem *Mayūrasandeśam* into Sanskrit, writes about Bharani Tirunal Lakshmi Bayi in such words:

> The princess who received instruction in Sanskrit in her childhood from her learned mother gradually grew up as a talented musician, poetess and water-colour painter. Her consort gave her instruction in Sanskrit classics and in turn she taught him music.
> (*Narayana Pillai 1984: 19*)

The *Mayūrasandeśa* is a messenger poem, which was written in very special circumstances. Kerala Varma and the Senior Rani were considered by King Ayiliyam Tirunal the allies of his younger brother, Viśakham[98] Tirunal Rama Varma. Finally, in 1875, Kerala Varma was arrested and Lakshmi Bayi's freedom restricted. The King compelled her to marry a second time and even chose the new bridegroom for her. "I have not yet become a widow to marry again" was her categorical reply (Narayana Pilllai 1984: 23).

The poem was written out of the poet's longing for the beloved wife. It is in line with the theoretical descriptions of the genre, which was quite popular in Kerala (Freeman 2003: 469–475,

---

[97] *Koṭṭāraṁ* (Mal.)—a royal residence, especially in Travancore.

[98] Mal. *viśākhaṃ* < Skt. *viśākhā*, i.e. the 14th, later 16th lunar asterism.

George 1968: 51–55), but the cause of its creation was provided by politics.

In the *Mayūrasandeśam*, the Senior Rani's husband says about her:

> *O, Peacock par excellence, as my beloved sings sweet devotional lyrics of her own composition in order to ease her heart of the agony of separation, your ears will spontaneously get themselves immersed for long in ocean of mirth.*
> (*Kerala Varma Koyil Tampuran 1984: 62, transl. P. K. Narayana Pillai*)

Only her works in Manipravalam[99] and Malayalam are available at present. Among her poems the devotional hymns such as the *Pārvatīstotra* are enumerated but there is also the *Virahiṇīpralāpa*, i.e. "Complaint of a lonely woman" (Narayana Pillai 1984: 19). It must be Lakshmi Bayi's expression of suffering. Thus, the couple separated for so long perhaps found consolation in composing literary works and in Rani's case also music. They were reunited in 1880, after the death of Ayiliyam Tirunal.

3. Other *svarupams*' women writers

Among younger and older contemporaries of the princesses mentioned above, there were many women well educated in Sanskrit and talented poetesses themselves, related to the Travancore Royal Family in fact in blood, although according to the matriliny rules not treated as relatives. They were sharing the same intellectual atmosphere of the royal court promoting talented poets and composers.

[99] Manipravalam (*maṇipravālam*)—a hybrid language, mixing, in the case of Kerala, Malayalam and Sanskrit.

3.1. Parappur Svarupam

Let us start with the family which finally settled in the Travancore Kingdom, namely the old royal house in South Malabar, Parappur Svarupam (Mal. *parappūr*). They ruled over their own country named Parappanad (Mal. *parappanāṭu˘*), which consisted of two parts: "the southern part included certain portions of the Tirūr̲ taluk,[100] while the northern part included Ce̲ruvaṇṇūr, Beypur̲ and Panniyaṅkara" (Ibrahimkunju 2007: 66). William Logan in his *Malabar Manual*, a monumental guide to the Malabar District under the Presidency of Madras in British India, provides such information about this noble family:

> Of *Rajputs*, or foreign Kshatriyas, there are in Malabar (census 1881) only three hundred and sixty-two all told. The families of the Kottayam and Parappanad chieftains belong to this class, and the former of these chieftains used sometimes to be called the *Puranatt* (i.e., foreign) Raja. The Parappanad family supplies consorts to the Ranis of Travancore, and also forms similar connections with the families of other chieftains in Malabar. They follow the *Marumakkatayam* law of inheritance.
> (*Logan 1951: 131*)

According to tradition, the abode of the kings was at Parappanangadi (Mal. *parappanaṅṅāṭi*), while the female line had the seat at Kadalundi (Mal. *kaṭaluṇṭi*). They had the palace or *kōvilakam* on a small hillock called Mekkotta (Mal. *mekkoṭṭa*), so the palace was known as the Mekkoṭṭayil Kōvilakam (Mal.). According to tradition, at a certain point in time the family consisted of three sisters, named Ambika (Mal. *ambika*, Skt. *ambikā*), Umamba (Mal. *umāmba*) and Ambadevi (Mal. *ambādēvi*). In the course of time, difference of opinion among the three sisters made them think about establishing their own *kōvilakams*. Finally, they left

[100] Taluk or tehsil—a name of an administrative unit, the sub-district in some of the states of India.

Kadalundi and the eldest sister, Ambika, created the Valu Kuriyedatu (Mal. *valu kuṟiyēṭatu*) Kovilakam in Neduva (Mal. *neḍuva*) near Parappanangadi.[101] The second sister, Umamba, established her *kōvilakam* near Calicut, in a place called Beypur. She named it Karippa Kovilakam. The third sister also migrated to Beypur and gave rise to Aliyakottu Kovilakam. She had two daughters named Lakshmi and Kunji (Mal. *kuññi*). Again Lakshmi and her children decided to move out of the Aliyakottu Kovilakam and she established in Beypur her own taravad known as Tattari Kovilakam (Mal. *tattāri kōvilakam*). Its members migrated to Travancore invited there. At the end of 1696, Umayamma Rani (Mal. *umayammarāṇi*; r. 1677–1684) adopted two princes and four princesses into the royal family.[102] The youngest among the

[101] "Ambika had a daughter called Ambadevi. Ambadevi begot a daughter named Amba. And Amba had a daughter, Umamba. This Umamba had four daughters—Lakshmi, Kunji, Unnikkutty and Ichamma. In the course of time, Lakshmi established a branch called *Valu Puthiya Kovilakom*. Lakshmi had two sons and six daughters. All of them including Lakshmi were adopted by the Kottayam Royal Family. The second daughter, Kunji, established her own place called *'Padinjaraypattu Kovilakom'*. The third daughter, Unnikkutty, established *'Padinjaray Kovilakom'*. This Kovilakom became extinct for want of female members to continue the line. Unnikkutty had one son only. During the invasion of Malabar by Tippu Sultan of Mysore in 1789 CE, all the members of the Valu Kuriyedathu Kovilakom, who were residing in their respective branch Kovilakoms, were captured by him and taken to Coimbatore and imprisoned. They were released only in 1792, following the Treaty at Seringapatam. But then, caste laws of those days had made them 'jātihīna' (outcastes) and they had to spend the rest of their days without social mingling with members of Hindu community or members of their families." (From the interviews and notes provided on 19th January 2014 and February 2015 by Dr. R. P. Raja, a son of C. K. Kerala Varma of Parappur Svarupam, Aliyakottu branch).

[102] Other authors speak about two princesses, of whom the elder died issueless and the younger one begot Martanda Varma; also the date of the adoption is different (e.g. Nagam Aiya 1906: 315, 332). The confusion with the number of adopted princesses and the date of the adoption can be explained by the fact mentioned by de Lannoy, that in 1687 the two princesses from the northern Malabar were sent for but "(...) it turned out that they were of a wrong

princesses became the mother of Martanda Varma, born in 1705 (De Lannoy 1997: 17). The newcomers to Travancore settlled down in the village of Kilimanur and their palace is known just as Kiḷimānūr Koṭṭāram.[103] This was the birthplace of many talented scholars and artists, a painter Raja Ravi Varma being the most well-known among them. In the year 1766, when Hyder Ali of Mysore entered the Bidnur country and attacked Malabar, Aliyakottu Kovilakam along with some others fled to Travancore seeking shelter under Karttika Tirunal Rama Varma known as Dharma Raja. Dharma Raja accommodated the Aliyakottu Kovilakam in Changanacherry, 20 kilometers south of Kottayam (Mal. *kōṭṭayaṃ*).

Thus by the last decade of the 17th century the Tattari Kovilakam and by 1766[104] the Aliyakottu Kovilakam became settlers in Travancore. Both branches are blood relatives of the Royal Family of Travancore as their sons were and are the consorts of Travancorean princesses.

3.2. Literary and scholarly achievements of Kilimanur Kovilakam ladies

> Kilimanur literally means "the land of the parrot and the deer". So wild was the country when the estate was granted. It is situated nearly seven miles to the north-east of Attungal, the seat of the Ranis and tventy-seven miles to the north of Trivandrum. (...)

---

branch of the royal house of Kolathiri. Because it would have been an offence to send them back, they were adopted into the house of one of the *pandara pillamar* (royal pages) (...)" (De Lannoy 1997: 14). Perhaps these arrivals of the princesses were mixed in some sources.

[103] Mal. *kiḷimānūr koṭṭāram*, *kōvilakam*=palace).

[104] In other sources the latter date is suggested, e.g.: "About 963 M.E., a fresh colony of Kōil Tampurāns arrived in Travancore, having run away to escape the oppresion of Tippu Sulṭān" (Padmanabha Menon 1993: 139–140). The date of Malayalam/Kollam Era 963 corresponds to 1788 CE.

> The Kilimanur Koil Tampurans are the native of Parappanad in Malabar. Their northern home is known as "Tattari-kovilakam". The great Martanda Varma Maharajah, the founder of Travancore, and his illustrious nephew Rama Varma, were the issue of the alliance with Kilimanur (...).
> (*Naga Aiya 1906: 329*)

In such a way Diwan Bahadur[105] V. Nagam Aiya (December 1850–1917), an Indian historian, civil servant and chronicler in the erstwhile princely state of Travancore, wrote about Kilimanur and its Koyil Tampurans. The Kilimanur Palace (Figs 10–11, p. 86) was the birthplace of many literati and artists, among them authoresses writing in Sanskrit, Manipravalam and Malayalam. Unfortunately, not too much has been preserved for the posterior generations; nevertheless, their names as great Sanskrit scholars are still present in the memory of the family members.

One of them is Umadevi Tampuratti, born in the year 1797. She was a sister of Raghava Varma Koyil Tampuran, the consort of Rani Gouri Parvati Bayi, who ruled Travancore as the regent until Svati Tirunal attained maturity. Umadevi was married to Kizhakkancherry Narayanan (Mal. *kiḻakkanśśēri nārāyaṇan*) Nambudiri, an expert in Vedas and *śāstras*, bearing the title of *bhāgavaṭottama*, i. e. someone who is able to read and explain the *Bhāgavatapurāṇa* within seven days as prescribed. She had fame in the family as a poetess writing both in Sanskrit and Malayalam. Perhaps it was due to her influence that her son Anizham[106] Raja Raja Varma, known in the family circles as Cherunni (Mal. *cēruṇṇi*), composed his first short Sanskrit poem at the age of nine (Raja 2006: 179–181). Later on he became a poet at the court

[105] Diwan Bahadur—title of honour during the British Raj. Diwan (*dīvān*), the word comes from Arabic and means "a royal court", "a prime minister"; *bahādur* comes from Persian and means "brave", "courageous", "invincible" or "a hero" (Hindi-English Dictionary, Pathak 1966: 519, 770).

[106] Mal. *aniḻam*; Skt. *anurādhā*—the seventeenth lunar mansion.

of Svati Tirunal. Makayiram[107] Nal Ambadevi Tampuratti also belonged to the Kilimanur Palace. She was born in 1832. She was a knowledgeable lady, writing Malayalam and Sanskrit works, a good musician and an expert Ayurvedic physician, specializing in *netracikitsā* (ophthalmology) and *bālacikitsā* (paediatrics). She used to compose hymns and prayers to different gods and goddesses but in the words of R. P. Raja: "no one bothered to record them and save them" (personal communication and notes I received in January 2014). The Kilimanur Tampurattis, although very well educated in Sanskrit, composed mainly in Malayalam, probably because they could get more readers in family circles and outside Kilimanur. Many of them studied and practised Ayurveda and for that purpose a good knowledge of Sanskrit was also important.

The present Valiya[108] Tampuratti (the senior female member of the family) Setu continues the tradition of Sanskrit learning in the family as she has translated *Śrīkṛṣṇavilāsam*,[109] a Sanskrit epic poem or *mahākāvya* in twelve chapters into Malayalam.

3.3. Aliyakottu Kovilakam

Aliyakottu Kovilakam, who was given shelter in the Travancorean kingdom and settled at the Niralikettu (Mal. *nīrāḻikēṭṭu*) Palace at Changanacherry, quite soon branched out again. When the family reached Travancore in 1766, it had a senior female member Kunjikutty (Mal. *kuññikuṭṭi*) and her five daughters: Ittotta, Ittiyangala, Njanji, Akkiyamma and Injnanji.

Ittotta established the Gramathil Kottaram, Ittiyangala and

---

[107] Mal. *makayiraṃ*, Skt. *mṛgaśīrṣa*—the 3rd or 5th lunar asterism containing three stars and visualized as an antelope's (*mṛga*) head (*śiras*).

[108] Mal. *valiya*—adjective: senior, grand, great.

[109] Kiḷimānūr Setu Tampurāṭṭi, (transl.) 2011. Sukumāra, *Śrīkṛṣṇavilāsam*. Kochi: Kurukshetra Prakasan.

Njanji brought to life the Paliyekkara[110] Kottaram at Tiruvalla,[111] Akkiyamma established the Pallom[112] Palace near Kottayam and Injnanji continued in Niralikkettu at Changanacherry. Injnanji's had a daughter, Attam[113] Tirunal Kunji (Mal. *kuññi*), who gave birth to a daughter Ittiyangala and a son, Raja Raja Varma, who fathered Svati Tirunal. Ittiyangala had three daughters, among whom Punartam[114] Nal Kunjikutty continued in Changanacherry in the Lakshmipuram Palace.[115] Punartam Nal Lakshmi moved to Harippad[116] and established the Anantapuram branch of the family and Punartam Nal Kochukunji (Mal. *koccukuññi*) established the Chemprol Kottaram (Figs 13–14, pp. 87–88) again in Harippad. In all the branches of the Aliyakottu Kovilakam there were women writers and scholars. Some of the ladies exhibited real litterary talents. For instance, Karttika Nal Ambadevi Tampuratti (b. 1878) of the Anantapuram Palace, Harippad, was a well-known Sanskrit scholar and the authoress of a number of literary works written in Sanskrit as well as in Malayalam. She translated a drama by Kodungallur Kunjikuttan (Mal. *kuññikuṭṭan*) Tampuran entitled *Candrikā* from Malayalam into Sanskrit. That fact was mentioned by Vadakkumkur Rajaraja Varma Raja in his

---

[110] Mal. *pāliyakkaṟa*. The Paliyekkara Palace was built by King Svati Tirunal of Travancore for his sister (Schildt 2012: 73). Henri Schildt in his monograph *The traditional Kerala Manor: Architecture of a South Indian Catuḥśāla House* provides plans, cross-sections and photos of this palace (Schildt 2012: 370–376).

[111] Mal. *tiruvaḷḷa*, a locality in central Travanacore.

[112] Mal. *pallōm*, a town in the Kottayam District.

[113] Mal. *attam*, Skt. *hasta*; the 11th or 13th lunar asterism, represented as a hand and containing five stars.

[114] Mal. *puṇartam*, Skt. *punarvasu*; the name of the 5th or 7th lunar mansion.

[115] Their seat Niralikettu was renamed to Lakshmipuram Kottaram in memory of Rani Gouri Lakshmi Bayi, who married a son of this family.

[116] Mal. *harippād*, sometimes Anglicized as Arippad, a place in northern Travancore, at present the Alleppey District.

six-volume *Kēraḷīyasaṃskṛtasāhityacaritraṃ* and because of that also noted down in the index of Kerala authors and their works in Sanskrit prepared by E. Easwaran Nampoothiry (Easwaran Nampoothiry 1972: 4).

Dr. R. P. Raja informed me that other ladies of the Anantapuram Palace also left literary legacy. He mentioned Puyam[117] Nal Ambalika[118] Tampuratti as an accomplished poetess writing in Sanskrit and Malayalam. She composed the *Rāmāyaṇasaṃgraha*; other works need to be traced. Also Trikketta[119] Nal Lalitamba Tampuratti composed in Sanskrit. Her *Gaṇeśacaritam* was published; the details should be traced.[120] Let us concentrate on the literary output of Ambadevi Tampuratti of the Chemprol Kottaram.

3.4. Ambadevi Tampuratti—her life and literary oeuvre[121]

Svati Tirunal Ambadevi Tampuratti (Fig. 3, p. 70) was born in the month of *mīnam* (Skt., Mal.; Pisces), on the 25th, in the Malabar year 1065, corresponding to 6th April, 1890 CE. Her mother was Trikketta Tirunal Kunjikutti and her father Brahmasri Krishnan Nambudiri belonged to Elangallur Mana.[122] She was married to Brahmasri Andaladi Divakaran Nambudiripad (Mal. *brahmaśrī andaladi divākaran nampūtirippāḍ*), a well-known scholar from Andaladi Mana, near Pattambi.[123] Ambadevi had five children:

[117] Mal. *pūyam*, Skt. *puṣya*—the 6th or 8th lunar asterism.

[118] Skt. *ambālikā*. Mal. *ambālika*.

[119] Mal. *trikkēṭṭa*, Skt. *jyeṣṭhā*—the 16th or 18th lunar mansion.

[120] Personal communication of Dr. R. P. Raja, 18th January 2014.

[121] This chapter is based on my article, Sudyka 2018a.

[122] Mal. *elaṅṅallūr mana*; Mal. mana=illaṃ—a house of Nambudiri Brahmins. Elangallur Mana is situated in the Kottayam District.

[123] Mal. *pattāmpi*, a town in the Palakkad District.

Revati[124] Tirunal C. K. Kerala Varma, Cittira Tirunal C. K. Raja Raja Varma, Aswati Tirunal Srimati Tampuratti, Visakham Tirunal C. K. Ravi Varma and Utram Tirunal C. K. Rama Varma.

Fig. 3. Svati Tirunal Ambadevi Tampuratti of the Chemprol Kottaram (1890–1928).

The mother of five children, who had previously received a thorough education at home, did not cease to be an expert and enthusiast of Sanskrit literature. She was still writing, both in Sanskrit and Malayalam, and teaching Sanskrit as well. Her son Visakham Tirunal C. K. Ravi Varma in his trip down memory lane mentions a Nambudiri neighbour, nearly as old as his mother, who "used to sit in the veranda and learn Sanskrit from mother sitting inside the adjacent room" (Raja 2012: 17).

Even this little note proves the fact that she maintained various social contacts. One of her visitors was, for example, a poet

[124] Mal. *rēvati*, Skt. *revatī*—the name of the fifth lunar mansion.

and journalist, Vennikkulam Gopala (Mal. gōpāla) Kurup (1902–1980).[125] As I have written in the article devoted to Ambadevi:

> He used to come frequently requesting for some write-ups from her. As the Keralan society was highly orthodox in its ideas of caste pollution, Vennikulam Gōpala Kurup could not enter the house, but waited at the door. Ambādēvi would give a note or her poem by dropping it into the hands of Gōpāla Kurup, for touching him would pollute her.
> (*Sudyka 2018: 190*)

As a poetess, then, she did not lead a secluded life. She communicated, as it is proved without any doubt, with at least one more poet, one of the so-called Great Trio of Malayalam poetry, the famous Vallattol Narayana Menon (16th October 1878–13th March 1958),[126] and made some contact with literary magazines, probably through Vallattol and Kurup, who published their own articles there. For example, the "Vanita Kusumam", a Malayali ladies' magazine, published her work *Śrībhūtanāthodaya* in parts. This magazine, along with some other ones, was an important instrument of creating an ambience for social reform movements at the end of the 19th and the beginning of the 20th centuries. As Teena Antony writes:

> In the 19th and early 20th centuries, women's magazines in Malayalam and other Indian languages provided opportunities for women writers and readers to express their opinions and debate issues that were related to their lives.
> (*Antony 2013: 20*)

These magazines published literary works not only of men but also of women writers. One of them was Ambadevi, who wrote

[125] See the entry concerning Kurup in *Encyclopaedia of Indian Literature: Devraj to Jyoti*, Vol. 2 (Datta, ed., 1988: 1445).

[126] Mal. *vaḷḷattōḷ nārāyaṇa mēnōn*. The other two poets are: Kumāran Āśān (1873–1924) and Uḷḷūr S. Paramēśvarayyar (1877–1949). See for example: George 1968: 147–159.

both in Malayalam and Sanskrit but only her two works in Malayalam were published. These are: the poem *Śrībhūtanāthodayam*, mentioned above, and the *Aṣṭamicampū*, which was a Malayalam translation of a Sanskrit work of the celebrated scholar and poet Melpputtur Narayana Bhatta.[127] Her other two Malayalam works—the *Ajāmilamokṣam* and the *Kanyakubjatilaykatha*—have never been published. The four poems, although written in vernacular, belong to Sanskrit literary culture. The story of Ajamila is described in the 6th canto of *Śrīmadbhāgavatam* and the stories from this *purāṇa* were eagerly retold over and over again, each time in a different form. In Kerala a very popular way of presenting the Puranic lore was through compositions in verse and prose, the so-called *campū prabandhas*, acted by a *cākyar*, hereditory actor of the Sanskrit dramas performed in the *kūṭiyaṭṭam* tradition. Also the story of Ajamila was represented in such a form. A very famous recapitulation of the sinful Brahmin Ajamila's story[128] was also provided by Melpputtur Narayana Bhatta (Śāstrī 1926: 295–300). The story of the origin of the name of the Kanyakubja city is known from the *Rāmāyaṇa* I.32. The *Śrībhūtanāthodayam* refers to Śiva, whereas the *Aṣṭamicampū* of Melpputtur Narayana Bhatta describes the *aṣṭami* festival as celebrated in Vaikkam in North Travancore (Kunjunni Raja 1980: 145).

Ambadevi was the author of many poems in Manipravalam and Sanskrit as well. Alas, now only one of them, a Sanskrit work, is available in fragments. This is the *Daśakumāracarita*, of which the following parts have been preserved:

---

[127] K. Kunjunni Raja devotes a whole chapter of his book *The Contribution of Kerala to Sanskrit Literature* to discuss his works and life (chapter "Nārāyaṇabhaṭṭa of Melputtūr" in: Kunjunni Raja, 1980: 119–152).

[128] Though he was only calling his son, even without any thought of god in his mind, Ajamila was saved because of repeating the name of god when the messengers of death were approaching him. The very uttering of God's name is enough for salvation. That is the message contained in the story.

Chapter II – from verse 294 to 385, Chapter III – 257 stanzas, Chapter IV – 161 stanzas, Chapter V – 127 stanzas, Chapter VI – 294 stanzas, Chapter VII – 131 stanzas, Chapter VIII – 281 and Conclusion – 68 stanzas (last stanza illegible).

Thus, the number of the preserved strophes is 1410 and the rest of the composition is lost to us.

The manuscript of her *Daśakumāracarita* has never been published. It was written in the Malayalam script on 44 pages of a notebook (Fig. 4, p. 73). Ambadevi sometimes added small cor-

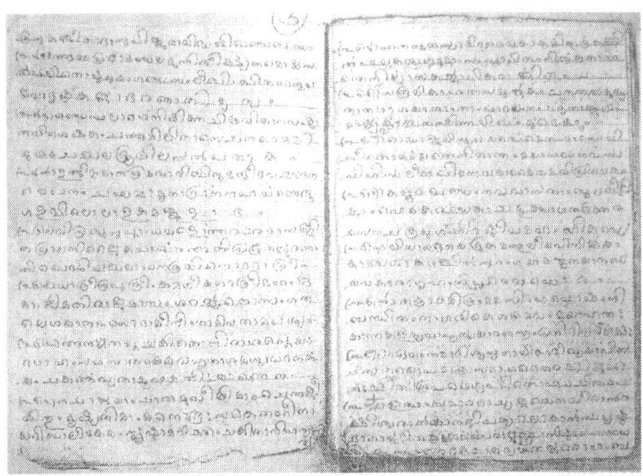

Fig. 4. A page from Svati Tirunal Ambadevi Tampuratti's *Daśakumāracarita* in her own handwriting.

rections above the line and postscripts in Malayalam, one of which we can find at the end of the second chapter. It informs us that the omitted verse 361 has been introduced at the very end, after the colophon finishing the chapter, i.e.*ucchvāsa*. As Ambadevi's son Visakham Tirunal C. K. Ravi Varma recalls, his mother "used to do all literary work in old notebooks, writing very closely with hardly any space between stanzas and paragraphs and using an ostrich feather pen and home prepared ink" (Raja, ed. 2012: 17).

Dr. R. P. Raja, a son of C. K. Kerala Varma of the Chemprol family, explains that:

> (...) those were times when writing material changed from cadjan leaves to paper. But then, paper or notebooks were not so easily available as it is today and so one had to scribble on whatever little paper or notebook that came one's way. And the case of Amba Devi was not different".[129]

Thus, one day, one of these old, ordinary looking notebooks might have been just thrown away.

On the other hand, the very intention of Ambadevi is unclear to us—she might have decided to restrict herself only to the part called by her the *Uttarapīṭhikā* or she might have wanted to incorporate also the *Pūrvapīṭhikā* into her poetic version of the *Daśakumāracarita*. The people of Kerala are known for their predilection for a melodious flow of poetry, which they learn by heart and recite with great enthusiasm. Ambadevi was acknowledged as an excellent Sanskrit scholar and as such, according to family tradition, she was asked to rewrite in verse the *Daśakumāracarita*, i.e. the "Adventures of ten young men", the famed prose work of Daṇḍin. Her rendering comprises different metres, typical of Sanskrit poetry, such as *vaṃśastha*, *anuṣṭubhśloka*, *triṣṭubh*, *mandākrantā*, *śikhariṇī*, *jagatī*, *sragdharā*, *upajāti*, to name only some of them.

Ambadevi's adaptation of Daṇḍin's prose masterpiece continues a long tradition followed by various other writers transforming this text. The original text itself has a quite complicated history and, alas, it has not been preserved in an intact form as the story lacks the beginning and ends abruptly. Perhaps this was the reason why several writers were ready to supplement its narrative.

Ketana (13th century CE), the author of the *Daśakumāracaritamu* in Telugu, was one of them. A. K. Warder believes that he

[129] R. P. Raja, notes prepared for the author, 8.01.2017.

takes credit for disseminating the text in its version as adventures of ten boys (Warder 1983: 167–169). Several incomplete and damaged manuscripts preserved in Kerala were used by M. R. Kavi to edit the *Avantisundarīkathā*, published in 1924; the restored text, however, had many lacunae. Some scholars are of the opinion that it contains the first part of Daṇḍin's work, but others deny Daṇḍin's authorship of the text edited as the *Avantisundarīkathā*.[130] Nonetheless, it is a long-established practice that Daṇḍin's masterpiece is presented as consisting of an opening—the *Pūrvapīṭhikā*,[131] normally comprising five chapters (called in Sanskrit *ucchvāsa*); followed by the part in eight *ucchvāsas* (6–13), by some scholars regarded as the only part composed by Daṇḍin and later known as the *Daśakumāracarita*; and concluded by the *Uttarapīṭhikā*, which is a short part, sometimes undivided, sometimes in two chapters (14–15).

Ambadevi's piece begins almost at the end of the second *ucchvāsa*. She finishes each *ucchvāsa* with a statement:

> *daśakumāracarite uttarapīṭhikāyāṁ dvitīya*
> *(tṛtīya, caturtha, etc.) ucchvāsas samāptaḥ /*
>
> The second (third, fourth etc.) chapter of *Uttarapīṭhikā*
> in the "Adventures of ten young men" has been finished.

It is obvious that the first chapter (*ucchvāsa*)[132] and 293 stanzas of the second one of her manuscript are missing. It is also highly

---

[130] Lienhard 1984: 236–237. The latest proposal of Herman Tieken aims at showing that all three parts of the text, which he calls a patchwork, form a close-knit frame story. He argues that "the cuts between the beginning, central part and ending are too neat to assume that the beginning and end were lost accidentally. Instead, the authors of the alternative beginnings and endings would have had access to the originals, which they replaced by their own, 'improved', versions" (Tieken 2013: 248). He also claims that Daṇḍin himself could author the *Pūrvapīṭhikā*.

[131] *pūrvapīṭhikā*— Skt. "introduction".

[132] The family claims that this first chapter contained 385 stanzas (notes prepared by R. P. Raja on 18th January 2014).

probable that Ambadevi Tampuratti wrote the *Pūrvapīṭhikā* after all, which can be concluded from the fact that she apparently planned two parts of her composition. The above-cited excerpt provides the reader with the information which particular chapter in the *Uttarapīṭhikā* finishes. The word *uttara* in Sanskrit means "later, following, subsequent, latter" and also "concluding" and we definitely have to take the meaning 'subsequent' into account while considering the existence of the first part. Ambadevi did not situate all the eight *ucchvāsas* in the central part of the text as was the usual practice, instead placing them in the section described as subsequent, which proves the fact that there must have been a part preceding it. In all probability, it might have been written down together with the first and the beginning of the second *ucchvāsa* in another, now lost notebook which she used for her writings. Yet another appearance of the word *uttarapīṭhikā*, this time in perfect agreement with the tradition of transmitting Daṇḍin's text which was described above, can be noted at the top of page 41d of her manuscript: here the word is used differently, as a title, and introduces the conclusion.

Let us now compare Ambadevi's version with Daṇḍin's original. We can see that she was quite successful both with the subject matter and with the form. She does not follow the plot slavishly, omitting parts of the description and some epithets; yet, she preserves the necessary contents for the story to flow smoothly. Her word choice sometimes agrees with that of Daṇḍin, other times she prefers synonyms, for example suiting the metre. For comparison, let us examine the beginning of the fourth chapter of "Adventures of ten young men":[133]

---

[133] I provide the appropriate Daṇḍin prose fragment for the sake of comparison:

> *deva, so 'ham apy ebhir eva suhṛdbhir ekakarmormimālinemibhūmivalayaṃ paribhramann upāsaraṃ kadācit kāśīpurīṃ vārāṇasīm /*
> *upaspṛśya maṇibhaṅganirmalāmbhasi maṇikarṇikāyām avimukteśvaraṃ bhagavantam andhakamathanam abhipraṇamya pradakṣiṇaṃ paribhraman puruṣam ekam āyāmavantam ā yasaparighapīvarābhyāṃ bhujābhyām*

suhṛd[em. t]bhir ebhir diśi diśy ahaṁ tu
paribhraman deva bhavā[em. a]didṛkṣuḥ /
kaśīpurīṁ tāpaharām kadācit
vārāṇasīm tāṁ samupāsaraṁ ca //(1)

Sire, wishing to see you,
I was roaming here and there with these friends.
Once I arrived at this City of Light,
which removes affliction—Varanasi.

vāriṇy upaspṛśya maṇiprakāśe
mahānubhāvaṁ maṇikarṇikāyāṁ /
natvāndhakārim bhagavantam ārāt
pradakṣiṇaṁ tatra cakāra so'haṁ // (2)

Having bathed in the crystal clear waters,
at the Manikarnika Ghat, after bowing before Lord Śiva,
the mighty enemy of demon Andhaka,
I immediately circumambulated this [temple].

āyāmavantaṁ paribaddhakakṣā-
bandhaṁ bhuj[em.bhubh]ābhyām atipīvarābhyāṁ /
atarkk[134] *ayaṁ pūruṣam ekṣya kañcit*
tadā sadākrandanatāmranetrāṁ // (3)

At that moment,
seeing a certain very tall man,
girding up his loins with his extremely massive arms
and with his eyes red due to incessant crying, I reflected:

Here we have three stanzas composed of four eleven-syllable quarters (*pāda*) each. They are all written in the so-called *upajāti* metre, a mixture of *upendravajrā* and *indravajrā pādas*, i.e. the quarters of a regular stanza. Nevertheless, the poetess applies different patterns to introduce both metres. Thus, in the first stanza

---

ābadhyamānaparikaram aviratarudito cchūnatāmradṛṣṭim adrākṣam /
atarkayaṃ ca-
(Kale, ed. 1986: 123).

[134] Doubled consonants are characteristic of this manuscript.

three *pādas* are in *upendravajrā* and the last one in *indravajrā*; in the second one *indravajrā* and *upendravajrā* alternate; whereas in the third one the first two *pādas* are in *indravajrā* and the last pair is in *upendravajrā*. Such an arrangement shows that the poetess carefully planned the application of metres. As far as the sound layer is concerned, she took also euphonic qualities into account, making use of alliteration in these stanzas. Describing Varanasi, she used the term *tāpaharā*, namely removing sorrows. Another word absent from the original prose text is the compound *bhavādidṛkṣu*, which is ambiguous, most probably in accordance with the intention of the poetess. I have suggested to emendate *bhava* to *bhavā*, both for metrical reasons and the logic of the narrative. It is also possible, however, that the poetess wanted to allude to the meanings brought by *bhava*, which not only denotes "worldly existence, the world, welfare", but also means Śiva as another name for Varanasi is the city of Śiva. We can also notice that Ambadevi's verses, without long sentences and very long compound words, are easier to comprehend as compared to Daṇḍin's prose. They are undoubtedly more melodious and thus much more worth the effort of memorising, which, supposedly, was the aim of such an undertaking.

The narrator of the story, like in Daṇḍin's prose work, describes what he sees and also what he thinks. After noticing a man of a powerful form, crying his eyes out (*cakṣur varṣaty ayaṁ kṣīṇakanīnikaṁ ca* – 4b), at the end of the fourth stanza he expresses his own guess: "At present he does not care about his life" (*nirāgraho nūnam asau nijāsau* – 4d) and can act and over-hastily and violently (*atisahāso 'sti*). Such is the beginning of Arthapāla's adventure, which will be narrated in metrical form by Ambadevi.

From the very small sample of her work we can conclude that her command of Sanskrit and knowledge of classical metres were excellent. It is regrettable, however, that we are not in the possession of her own independent works, which would certainly show her own poetical imagination.

Svati Tirunal Ambadevi Tampuratti died, following a short illness, on the 26th of *makaram*, 1103 M.E. (Malabar Era) corresponding to 8th February, 1928, at the age of 38. During her lifetime, like any other woman, she was forced by harsh orthodoxy to follow many restrictions. There was almost no way for a woman to announce to the world her achievements or even mastery in the field of literature, science or art. The knowledge of their possible successes was limited to the family circles and, like them, almost closed within the four walls of their homes. Seldom could their reputation as good scholars, artists or writers reach a wider audience. Dr. R. P. Raja, Ambadevi's blood relative, is convinced that it is still possible to recover some manuscripts written by women as they may lay hidden not only in royal residences but in Brahmin, Nayar and Ezhava homes in all Kerala. However, it would require very hard and systematic efforts. Ambadevi's case was different in such respect that some of her poems in Malayalam were published during her lifetime and her talent and knowledge recognised. When she died, the "Vanita Kusumam" magazine published an obituary announcing her death. Ullur S. Paramesvarayyar in his well-known history of literature, the *Keralasāhityacaritram*, mentions her name and titles of her works, and so does Vadakkumkur Rajaraja Varma Raja in the *Keralīyasamskṛtasāhityacaritram*. Easwaran Nampoothiry's Sanskrit index of authors and their works also records them (Easwaran Nampoothiry 1972: 4). The next step should be the publication of her *Daśakumāracarita*, luckily preserved by her family. Such an endeavour would not only distinctly testify to the skills and knowledge of a woman writing in Sanskrit at the beginning of the 20th century and to the continuous Sanskrit tradition in Kerala at that time, but also significantly contribute to the reception of the *Daśakumāracarita* itself.

3.5. Asvati Tirunal Srimati Tampuratti of Chemprol Kottaram

She was a daughter of Svati Tirunal Ambadevi Tampuratti, an equally talented poetess, both in Sanskrit and Malayalam. A sudden tragedy in her life burnt out her enthusiasm for writing. Only a very occasional sprouts appeared. She wrote the *Harigītapureśa-suprabhātam* in Sanskrit and many incidental verses. The family tells stories about instances of poetry produced by her extempore. When asked by her grandson, Prince Asvati Nal Rama Varma, about a poem to celebrate the 60th birthday (*ṣaṣṭipūrti*) of a famous music maestro Sri Semmankudi Sreenivasa Iyer, she took an old envelope, as there was nothing else at hand at that moment, and tearing it open she wrote a small laudatory poem in Malayalam. Realizing that in Tamil Nadu possibly no one would be able to appreciate poetry in Malayalam, she immediately rendered it into Sanskrit.

Her son, Sri Chemprol Raja Raja Varma, remembers his mother saying that writing in Sanskrit is easier than in Malayalam because of the vastness of synonyms. The richness of synonyms in Sanskrit, she claimed, allows a poet to select the variant suitable for the metre and other artistic effects which the author wanted to achieve. Her mother, Svati Tirunal Ambadevi Tampuratti wrote with equal easiness both in Malayalam and Sanskrit but she considered herself rather a Sanskrit poet.[135]

3.6. Amma Vidus

Amma Vidu or "the house of a royal spouse" could provide also an ambience in which the girls could receive good education and become a writer. Here the well-known case is Kuttikunju (Mal.

[135] Personal communication with Sri Chemprol Raja Raja Varma, February 2014.

kuṭṭikuñcu) Tankachi born in 1820. She was a daughter of Irayimman Tambi, a famous poet and composer.[136] Irayimman Tambi married his uncle's daughter Kalipilla (Mal. *kālipiḷḷa*) Tankachi. Their daughter Kuttikunju received her early education in Sanskrit under Harippad Kochu Pilla Warrier (Mal. *koccu piḷḷa vāriyar*). Higher education was implemented by her father. She wrote eighteen works, among them three play texts, i.e. *āṭṭakathas* for the dance-drama of Kerala, namely *kathakaḷi*. In the *āṭṭakathas*, although written in Malayalam, there are stanzas in Sanskrit.[137] These verses connect the whole story. The following *kathakaḷi* texts were written by Kuttikunju: the *Śrīmatisvayaṃvaram*, *Pārvatīsvayaṃvaram* and *Mitrasahamokṣam*. Her Manipravalam work is the *Kalyāṇaghoṣam*.[138] Kuttikunju's younger contemporary was Kalyanikutti (Mal. *kalyāṇikuṭṭi*) Ammachi of Nagercoil Amma Vidu, who was born in 1839. She composed poems in Sanskrit, Manipravalam and Malayalam. In Sanskrit she wrote for instance the *Stavamallikā*. In fact, Kalyani was adopted to the Nagercoil Amma Vidu, as King Ayiliyam Tirunal wanted to marry her. Her colourful life could become canvas for a novel. Ayiliyam Tirunal dissolved her earlier marriage with a famous *kathakaḷi* actor and in 1862 she became the royal consort. As Manu S. Pillai writes:

> Slowly a coterie of young intellectuals, artists, musicians, and others began to revolve around her, a fine poet and composer of Sanskrit

[136] Irayimman Tambi's mother was Parvati Pilla Tankachi, a second daughter of Makayiram Tirunal Ravi Varma, Elaya Tampuran (heir apparent; Mal. *iḷaya*—junior) of Travancore. More about Irayimman Tambi, his compositions, his family and roots of Amma Vidus in: Raja 2014. I am thankful to the author of the monography on Irayimman Tambi for sharing his knowledge about Irayimman's daughter, Kuttikunju.

[137] About *kathakaḷi* read for instance in Zarrilli 2007.

[138] S. Guptan Nair (22 August 1919—6 February 2006), an Indian scholar, academic, critic and writer, in 1979 edited a book devoted to Kuttikunju Tankachi published by Kerala Sahitya Akademi. That is why the knowledge about her has reached a wider audience in Kerala.

> plays herself, and her obliging husband. She went on to learn English, even interacting with Christian missionaries and reading the Bible, with an urbane irreverence that at once attracted and infuriated less liberal souls outside her ring.
> (*Pillai 2015: 33*)

In conclusion, it can be stated that in Travancore among royalty as well as in aristocratic families linked to the Travanacorean court there were women who were recognised as brilliant Sanskrit scholars and talented poets. Some of them had strong personalities, were noticed and valued for their literary talents, as did Ambadevi of Chemprol Kottaram and Kuttikunju Tankachi, and their opinions on literature-related topics mattered. The knowledge of the talents of others have not gone beyond family circles.

Fig. 5. Map of Travancore, Cochin and Malabar. Source: Constable's Hand Atlas of India, Section XIV, plate 35, 1893.

Fig. 6. Narendra Printers at Mannadiar Lane in Trichur in 2005.

Fig. 7. Padmanabhapuram Palace.

Fig. 8. Padmanabhapuram Palace.

Fig. 9. Dharma Raja's picture from the Padmanabha Palace.

Fig. 10. Kilimanur Palace.

Fig. 11. Kilimanur Palace.

Fig. 12. Performance Hall (Skt. *nāṭakaśālā*) in Kilimanur.

Fig. 13. Chemprol Kottaram, Harippad.

Fig. 14. Chemprol Kottaram, Harippad.

III. Singing the Glory of the Gods. Makayiram Nal Amba Tampuratti of Punjar

1. The history of Punjar Rajas

1.1. The Pandyas of Madurai come to Kerala. A Chronicle of the beginnings of the Punjar Kingdom

The accounts of this house and the memory of its members passed from one generation to another point to Madurai as their native place and the Pandya (Skt. *pāṇḍya*, Tam. pāṇṭiyar) kings as their ancestors. As family tradition has it,[139] at the time of Kulottunga II Chola's (*kulottuṅga*) reign (1135–1150), Prince Chirayu Varma (Skt. *cirāyuvarman*) of the Pandya dynasty, after turning eighteen, became the ruler of Madurai. The brave young king could not accept the suzerainty of the Cholas over the Pandya region and routed a Chola army contingent out of Madurai. Enraged Kulottunga Chola invaded Madurai with a large army. Finding that his commander-in-chief had changed sides after receiving a lot of money from the Cholas, Chirayu realized that it was futile

[139] The account is given in the *Pūññāṟ rājakuṭumba caritrāvalōkanam* authored by Sri P. R. Rama Varma Raja, late Valiya Raja, i.e. head of the Punjar family (Rama Varma Raja 1988).

to try resisting the Chola King with his disarrayed army. Thus the king with his family moved out of Madurai and went to Gudalur, situated in the Western Ghats region, close to Kerala.[140] He took the *utsavavigrahas* (Skt.), i.e. the idols used during the festival processions, of the family deity Mīnākṣī (Skt.) and that of Sundareśvara (Skt.) along with him. He also emptied his treasury and carried away all valuables. After reaching Gudalur, he established a domain of the Pandyas (Skt. *pāndyamaṇḍalam*) there. His younger brother Maravarman Srivallabhan (Tam. *māravarmaṉ srīvallabhaṉ*) (1132–1161?) ruled in the Pandya country.[141] In the course of time, friendly relations became established between Chirayu and the Cholas. The Cholas honoured him with the title Manavikrama (Skt. *mānavikrama*), and Chirayu Varma, in turn, began using this name. While he continued living at Gudalur, he came to know that on payment of money lands were available in Kerala from the ruler of Tekkumkur, whose capital was at Kottayam. Learning also about the fertility of the Kerala region, Manavikraman wanted to own those lands both for increasing his revenue as well as to expand his kingdom. With this intent, the king himself undertook a journey, along with a retinue of soldiers for security reasons, and began to climb the mountains and cross the dense jungles of the Western Ghats. He travelled through the mountain passes of Kumily (Mal. *kumaḷi*) and Idukki (Mal. *iṭukki*). While Manavikraman was camping, a gang of thieves attacked his camp. Though he had his soldiers

[140] There are two localities in Tamil Nadu bearing this name: in the current Nilgiri District and in the Coimbatore District.

[141] There are doubts about the dates and details of his rule. Sethuraman claims that Maravarman could have ascended the throne as late as 1145–46 (Sethuraman 1980: 111). As Nilakanta Sastri notices, Maravarman was established in Tinnevelly (Nilakanta Sastri 1929: 128), which could have meant that, in the words of Nilakanta Sastri, "a rival prince" was occupating Madurai. Or was it his brother, who ruled from Madurai? Nowhere is the name of Chirayu mentioned.

with him, the bandits almost outnumbered them. But still, the king began to put up stiff resistance. While the fight was going on, a teenage boy, with a group of his own men, suddenly appeared on the scene riding an elephant. In no time was he able to defeat the gang, who, frightened by the unexpected attack, ran away. The boy approached Manavikraman, offfered him the elephant together with a goad (Mal. *tōṭṭi*) and a cane (Mal. *vaṭi*) to control the animal and informed the king that soon the same gang would attack the famous Śiva temple at Ettumanur (Mal. *ēṟṟumānūr*). He advised the king to protect the temple and disappeared. The king continued his journey and finally reached Ettumanur on the third day. As advised by the young man, the king and his retinue of soldiers stayed in secret inside the Ettumanur Temple. Around midnight, the gang attacked the Ettumanur Temple to plunder its treasury. But the sudden and unexpected attack by Manavikraman's soldiers frightened the head of the gang and he and what was left of his band fled from the place. The local population, learning what happened at night, became overjoyed at the saving of their temple and, thanking king Manavikraman, took him to their king, the ruler of Tekkumkur. The king of Tekkumkur was also very much pleased with the brave action of Manavikraman and enquired of him how he could help him. Manvikraman asked for some land, expressing his wish to buy it. The king of Tekkumkur agreed. Manavikraman paid the Tekkumkur king the price in valuable jewels, gold and money and bought a kingdom for himself. This and later purchases formed the area of the Punjar Kingdom in the Kerala region. Manavikraman had almost an equal amount of land in Gudalur also. Both the regions, those in Kerala and those in Tamil Nadu (*pāndyamaṇḍalam*) began to be ruled by the descendants of Manavikraman.

At first, the king settled his family in a place called Kanjirappally (Mal. *kāññirappaḷḷi*). While Chirayu Varma left Madurai, he carried the family deities along with him. At Kanjirappaly he built a shrine and worshipped them there. However, finally, he selected Punjar as his permanent seat. He firmly believed that the teenage boy who saved him out of bandits' hands was none other than an incarnation of Śrī Dharma Śāstā. The king wanted to construct a temple for Dharma Śāstā but could not decide on the location. There are two legends related to the establishment of the temple. One says that as the king went to the river for his daily bath, he had with him the *tōṭṭi* and *vaṭi* received from the mysterious boy. Before entering the river, he placed both on the ground near the shore. After the bath, the king came back and when he tried to lift the two objects, he could not do it. The king then realized that the Lord had shown him the location where the temple should be built. Another version is that it was an umbrella that the king placed on the ground. In accordance with the sign, which he believed to be divine in nature, Chirayu Varma built a temple for Śrī Dharma Śāstā, today known as Sri Dharma Sastha Kshetra of Punjar (Fig. 15, p. 105).

When the family became settled in Punjar, the idols of Madurai Mīnākṣī and Sundareśvara were brought from Kanjirappally[142] and kept in the shrine inside the palace complex, built in the traditional Kerala manner.[143] Some time after the construction of the Dharma Śāstā temple, a shrine was also constructed for the Madurai Mīnākṣī and Sundareśvara. That is the Madhura Meenakshi Temple of Punjar (Figs 16–17, pp. 105–106) as it is known today.[144] The scions of the Pandya royal dynasty from Madurai who first migrated to Gudalur and then became settled in Punjar built the Punjar Koyikkal (Mal. *kōyikkaḷ*) palace there, adopted local habits and took as their emblem *śrīcakra* from the Gudalur

[142] In Kanjirappally, there was, and still is, the temple constructed by the king where both idols were installed.

[143] This traditional architecture, called *nālukeṭṭu˘* (Mal.), is a structure consisting of four (Mal. *nālu*) houses (Mal. *nālukeṭṭu˘*) and an inner courtyard in the middle.

[144] See the website: http://koickaldevaswom.com.

temple with the images of a goad and cane given by the divine boy on both its sides.

According to some other versions of the story, as for instance noted down by Padmanabha Menon (1993: 85–91), Manavikrama, after diserting from Madurai, lived with the family in Palghat, then in Karikat Gramama (*kārikātgrāmam*) and some other places. The newcomers were not welcomed as the local rulers were afraid that they could be their rivals seeking their own kingdom. During this exile, while at the Edappally King's court, Manavikrama died. Soon his wife followed him. The princes-wanderers were asked by Edappally Raja to stay in Kochi[145] and their sister was wedded to Raja. Padmanabha Menon, presenting the whole history, rightly highlights a very interesting fact that it was a local type of marriage, i.e. *keṭṭukalyāṇam*, and the funeral rites for the dismissed Manavikrama and his wife were conducted by the sons of his sister. It clearly shows that the family adopted local customs. Twelve years later Edappally Raja died and his successor was not so friendly towards foreigners. The princes once again moved from their palace thinking about settling down close to their ancestral country. When they reached Vadakkumkur, they heard that the Raja ruling over the country called Punjar had been murdered. The eldest prince, bearing also the name of Manavikrama Kulashekhara Perumal, negotiated with Tekkumkur Raja named Aditya Varma (Skt. *ādityavarman*) and finally he purchased the Punjar country with valuables brought from the Pandya land. The transfer of all the rights to the kingdom was inscribed on a copper plate in the presence of witnesses. With the consent of inhabitants of the country Raja was installed on the throne. One can question the historicity of such legendary accounts but certain elements of the story speak for the fact that the Manavikrama family moved from Madurai and settled on the banks of the beautiful river Meenachil/Mīnaccil and stayed there. The

[145] Cochin, Anglicized form < Mal. Kocci.

river is also known as Punya from which the name *pūññāṟ*[146] originated. While travelling, they were "stamping" the area of their journey with the temples, which were a kind of replica of those from Madurai. In Gudalur there is the Aḻakar Svāmi temple traditionally connected with the Punjar Rajas and perhaps reproducing the Madurai Kūṭal Aḻakar temple, which lies one kilometer to the southwest of the Mīnākṣī-Sundareśvara temple complex.[147] As was mentioned above, the wandering Pandyas built the Mīnākṣī-Sundareśvara temples in their new locations, namely in Kanjirappally and Punjar. It looks as if the settlers replicated at least a part of the sacred geography of Madurai, "taming" the new region with the help of their gods. At Punjar they also built the Dharma Śāstā temple and Śāstā's cult, which, although present in Tamil Nadu as well, was particularly well developed in Kerala. So the family tradition, i.e. devotion towards the Goddess Mīnākṣī and Sundareśvara was broadened by adding a cult of a god who as is believed helped the newcomers to find the proper place to establish their capital.[148]

At the beginning of the 17th century, the Punjar Royal Family faced extinction. The then Punjar Raja adopted members of a family called Sarkkara Kovilakam from Venkitangu (Mal. *vēṅkiṭaṅgu*), a village near Guruvayur (Mal. *guruvāyūr*). They were also supposed to be the descendants of the Pandyas but

[146] Mal. *āṟ*—river.

[147] The Madurai Kūṭal Aḻakar temple as the present structure most probably comes from the mid-sixteenth century but "there was undoubtedly an earlier temple on the site, perhaps dating from the tenth or eleventh century (...) (Branfoot 2000: 200).

[148] Additionally, the legends of the tribes living in the hilly forests of the Punjar area seem to confirm the story. "The Mannāns are a hill tribe of Travancore, and are said to have been originally dependents of the kings of Madura, whom they, like the Ūrālis and Muduvans, accompanied to Nēriyamangalam" (Thurston Rangachari 1909: 452). See also Iyer 1937: 203 and Varghese 2018: 48.

migrated earlier and by that time amalgamated with the higher strata of the Keralan society and were treated as Kerala *kṣatriyas*. There is also another royal house, Pandalam (Mal. *pantaḷam*), which traces its beginning from the Pandya kings of Madurai. The migrants established "(...) a very small principality in the present Chengannur taluk" (Sreedhara Menon 2014: 165). Perhaps the parts of different histories of Pandyan migrations, in the case of the narrative told above showing the past of the Punjar Royal Family, merged or influenced each other producing versions differing one from the other.

Remembering the story of their descent, constituting the vital part of their identity, the Punjar Royal Family worship Mīnākṣi and Sundareśvara Svāmi. When a new king assumed the kingship, he went to that temple to take an oath before the Goddess that he would rule the kingdom justly and for the welfare of the people. However, their religious and communal rites and rituals are that of Kerala *kṣatriyas*. They adopted the Nambudiri Brahmins as their priests and practised the *anuloma*[149] form of marriage. The ladies of the Punjar family were married only to the Nambudiri Brahmins in the past. Thus till the middle of the 20th century all the members of the Punjar Royal Family were the children of the Nambudiri Brahmins. The Punjar Rajas story is an extremely interesting account about acculturation, assimilation and finding the right place in the new world. The last goal was achieved through buying the kingdom (this element appears in all versions), which is quite unusual. Usurping the thrones is definitely more frequently met with. The matrimonial alliances with *nampūtiris* and their role as family priests could help in legitimization of the rule of the newcomers.

[149] *anuloma* (Skt.)—a marriage in which a woman is of a lower caste than a man.

1.2. The Principality of Punjar

We have seen that originally Punjar was an independent kingdom extending both in Kerala and Tamil Nadu. In the march of time and history, the lands in Tamil Nadu were lost to the English East India Company. The Kerala area was also diminished through many treaties made both by the English and the Travancore Government. In 1749–50, after the annexation of Tekkumkur and Vadakkumkur by Martanda Varma, Punjar Rajas also became subjects of Travanacore (Sreedhara Menon 2014: 166). The erstwhile kingdom was reduced to an *iṭavaka*, i.e.principality. This area was ruled by the Punjar Chief. There was a court and other basic paraphernalia of an administrative unit. This status of principality was also lost due to land reform in Kerla.

Not much has been written about the history of the Punjar kingdom or principality. In *A Survey of Kerala History* by Sreedhara Menon this is less than one page altogether, finishing with the mention about the release of High Ranges (540 sq. kms) to an English tea planter John Daniel Munro signed by Kerala Varma Valiya Raja of Punjar on the 11th July 1887 (Sreedhara Menon 2014: 164).

At the beginning of the 20th century, in the main branch of the Punjar Royal Family, there were three sisters named Makayiram Nal Ambalika Tampuratti, Rohini[150] Nal Ambika Tampuratti and Karttika Nal Amba Tampuratti.[151] Traditionally, only three names were used for the ladies of this family. They were Amba, Ambika and Ambalika.[152] The sisters had an elder brother

[150] Mal. *rōhiṇi*, Skt. *rohiṇī*—the ninth of 27 *nakṣatras* or lunar mansion.

[151] Personal communication received from the members of the family during my visit to Punjar in February 2015.

[152] In the Sanskrit epic the *Mahābhārata* the three daughters of the king of Kāśi (Skt.) were named Ambā, Ambikā and Ambālikā.

Mulam[153] Nal Rama Varma, known among family member as Kochukunjunni (Mal. *koccukuññuṇṇi*) Tampuran. He, out of great affection for his sisters, bought some lands for them. He gave four and a half acres each to the two elder sisters and five acres to the youngest one. The youngest sister received more land because it was more arid and rocky than the other pieces. As years progressed, the joint family was growing bigger and bigger. When overcrowding was felt by the youngest sister, she decided to move to the place bought by her brother. Karttika Nal Amba Thampuratti was married to Brahmasri Narayanan Nambudiri of Putusseri (Mal. *putuśśēri*) Mana, a very dedicated scholar but also a bold and enterprising man.

When Amba Tampuratti decided to shift to her own place, a small house (Fig. 18, p. 106) was built on the top of the small hill with three rooms, one kitchen and verandas around it. They moved around 1933–34.

> Gradually, the original small building to where Karthika Thirunal Amba Thamburatty and children shifted came to be known as the '*Pazhaya Kettitam*' (old building). It was so, because, the eldest son of Amba Thamburatty, Sri P. R. Rama Varma Raja, built a new building on the hill top. The present Kanjiramattom is that building. The architect of that building was none other than Amba Thamburatty's another son, R. V. Raja (Belhavan Thirumeni). (...) The 'house warming' (*paalukachu*) of the building took place in 1937.
> (*Raja & Raja 2017: 136*)

In the middle room of the old building, there are pictures of ancestors and gods. In the north eastern corner a small shrine was built, where daily *pūjās* are conducted.

Karttika Tirunal Amba Tampuratti (Fig. 19, p. 107) and Putusseri Narayanan Namubudiri (Fig. 20, p. 107) had ten chil-

153 (Skt.) *mūla*, Mal.—the 17th or 19th lunar mansion.

dren: Avittam Nal Rama Varma, Karttika Nal Goda Varma,[154] Utradam[155] Nal Ambalika (married to Osseri Padmanabhan Nambudiri), Tiruvatira[156] Nal Rama Varma, **Makayiram Nal Amba** (married to Kodanad[157] Narayanan Nambudiripad; Figs 21–22, p. 108), Trikketta[158] Goda Varma, Puram[159] Nal Kerala Varma, Mulam Nal Rama Varma, Attam Nal Ambika (married to Captain Kerala Varma of the Cochin Royal Family) and Utram Amba (married to Ravi Varma of the Cochin Royal Family). The first male child in the family was traditionally given the name Rama Varma, whereas the second son was named Goda. The next male child could be named Kerala Varma. As can be noticed both youngest daughters of Karttika Tirunal Amba were not married to Nambudiris. At that time, in different social and economic situations, the traditional pattern changed. The marriages within the Tampurans community so far present in the Travancore Royal Family were extended to other royal bloods.

It was Makayiram Amba whose son Rama Varma became the Valiya Raja of the Punjar Family but of utmost importance for us is the fact that she was a Sanskrit scholar and some of her writings in Sanskrit have been preserved and even published by the family.

---

[154] Colonel Goda Varma married the First Princess of Travancore, Kartika Tirunal Lakshmi Bayi. He promoted sports, that is why his birthday, 13 October, is observed as Kerala Sports Day. More about his life and death in *Oru "tīrthayātra"* (A "Pilgrimage") by P. K. R. V. Raja and P. A. G. V. Raja, published in Punjar in 2017 and containing memories of other members of the family.

[155] Mal. *utrāṭam*, Skt. *uttarāṣaḍhā*—a name of the 21st lunar mansion.

[156] Mal. *tiruvāttira/ ātira*, Skt. *ārdrā*—the fourth or sixth lunar mansion.

[157] Mal. *kōṭanāṭŭ*—a riverside village in the Ernakulam district.

[158] Mal. *trikkēṭṭa/kēṭṭa*, Skt. *jyeṣṭha*—the 16th or 18th lunar mansion, sacred to god Indra.

[159] Mal. *pūram*, Skt. *pūrva/ pūrvaphalgunī*—the name of the 11th lunar mansion.

2. Makayiram Nal Amba Tampuratti—the Poetess

Amba was born in 1917 in the Punjar Royal Family's ancestral house Koyikkal (Figs 23–24, p. 109). She moved from the old family seat to the new place in 1934, then to Kanijiramattam palace (Fig. 25, p. 110) in 1937 along with her parents, brothers and sisters. She remained there till the end of her life in 2010.

After *vidyārambha*, Kunjananiti (Mal. *kuññananīti*), as she was called by the family members, started her early education learning the Malayalam script from family members. She did her primary schooling till the fourth class in the school set up for the royal family members. After the fourth class, she was not sent for higher education in a regular school, since girls were not sent to public institutions in those days. An eminent teacher in Sanskrit, Krishna Sastri (Skt. *kṛṣṇa śāstri*) from Palakkad (Mal. *pālakkāṭu˘*), was appointed to teach Sanskrit to the children in Koyikkal and she received her education in Sanskrit along with the other children of the family. Another teacher, a certain Krishnan (Mal. *kṛṣṇan*) belonging to Thiruvarppu (Mal. *tiruvarppu*) in Kottayam, was appointed to teach them music. Her eldest brother, Avittam Nal P. R. Rama Varma Raja, graduated from Presidency College, Madras, and took great interest in teaching his sisters English, which was how she learned the language. She developed a great interest, indeed a fascination for reading and pored over books of prose and especially poems in Malayalam and to some extent in Sanskrit. She had a prodigious memory and she often used to recite the various poems which she had learnt by heart.

Traditionally, martial arts and other exercises were also a part of education for boys as well as girls. There was a special place for that, i.e. *kaḷari* (Mal.), at Kanjiramattam, where children were trained by one Raman Asan. Perhaps the training was not as interesting for Amba as it became for her sister Attam Nal Ambika called Aniti, now the Valiya Tampuratti of Punjar, who had learnt some of the techniques, for instance fighting with a stick (Raja & Raja 2017: 143). Amba's interest in poetic creation seems to have flourished when she reached middle age as her attempts at poetry are preserved only from that period. It may have been the result of her health problems that started quite early when her vision deteriorated, which, nonetheless, never stopped her from reading, and then her hearing began to fail.[160] Perhaps she found retreat in her inner world, transforming her thoughts into poetry. Her works reflect deep devotion, which she also showed in organizing various religious rites and rituals. Her 84th birthday was commemorated by publishing her *Rāmāyaṇastuti*. It was printed in Punjar in 2001, in the form of a small booklet. The work was written in Sanskrit but, as was a normal practice for Keralan writers, in the Malayalam script (Fig. 26, p. 110). The composition transcends the generic conventions observed in Indian *kāvya* literature with its narrative structure and its peculiar form. There are seven chapters just like seven books in Vālmīki's *Rāmāyaṇa*. The names of the first six are exactly as those of the *Rāmāyaṇa*,[161] that is: *Bālakāṇḍa* (29 stanzas), *Ayodhyākāṇḍa* (39 stanzas), *Araṇyakāṇḍa* (52 stanzas), *Kiṣkindhākāṇḍa* (43 stanzas), *Sundarakāṇḍa* (76 stanzas) and *Yuddhakāṇḍa* (115 stanzas). The last chapter is entitled *Uttararāmacaritam* (87 stanzas), perhaps referring to the famous drama of Bhavabhūti (Skt.). Additionally, in accordance with the title of Amba's work, it is supposed to be a *stuti* and in the very first stanza she declares:

[160] All pieces of information come from the members of the Punjar Royal Family. I am grateful to P. A. Goda Varma Raja and his family for the invite to Punjar in 2015, where I was shown the Koyikal and Kanjiramattam palaces, and also for the hospitality I received during my short stay there.

[161] This is one of the reasons why the poem of Amba cannot be considered as a *mahākāvya*, also called *sargabandha*, i.e. consisting of *sargas*. These *sargas* should contain different descriptions and discursive passages and other elements pointed out by theoreticians of Sanskrit literature such as Daṇḍin, for example. Amba's poem lacks most of these elements but still it is a work of considerable length.

rāmāyaṇakathāsāraṁ
stotraṁ karttum ihodyatām
bhaktāṁ mām anugṛhṇīṣva
rāmacandranamo stute //1//

O Rāmacandra, bless me,
who am devoted to you and
ready to compose the prayer
being a summary of the *Rāmāyaṇa* story.
Salutations to you!

Each chapter finishes in a similar way as for example in the fourth chapter:

kiṣkindhākāṇḍarūpaṁ te
stotraṁ pādāṁbujarppitaṁ
bhaktisaṁvarddhakaṁ bhūyāt
sadā sajjanasammatam //43//

Let this *stotra* in the shape of the *Book of Kiṣkindhā*,
placed at your lotus feet,
increasing devotion to you,
be always thought highly of by good people.

With this work Makayiram Nal Amba Tampuratti finds her place among the many authors cultivating the long tradition of summarizing huge works such as the *Rāmāyaṇa* and *Mahābhārata*.[162] However, although Amba relates Rāma's adventures verse by verse, chapter by chapter, its form is quite exceptional. Each stanza of her narration finishes in the manner of a litany: "I seek refuge in Raghava" (*taṁ rāghavam āśrayāmi*), "I resort to Rāghava" (*rāghavaṁ bhaje*), "Oh Hari, salutation to you" (*hare namas te*), "I always bow to Rāma" (*rāmaṁ satataṁ namāmi*), "I praise Raghunātha" (*raghunātham īḍe*), "Oh God, salutation to you" (*bhagavan namas te*), "I constantly bow to noble Rāma's feet"

[162] It is worth mentioning that there is an extensive *Rāmāyaṇasāra* authored by a woman, Madhuravāṇī (Skt.), who lived at the court of Raghunatha Nayaka (Skt. *raghunāthanāyaka*; r. 1600–1634) (Sudyka 2013: 28, 201).

(*śrīrāmapādau satataṁ namāmi*), "I constantly take refuge with noble Rāmacandra" (*śrīrāmacandram aniśaṁ śaraṇaṁ prapadye*), "Let noble Rāma protect always" (*śrīrāmaḥ sarvadāvatu*), etc. At the end of each stanza the authoress asks Rāma to take care of the world or expresses her devotion to God. Sometimes she even repeats the same phrase in the last *pādas* (quarters) of several consecutive stanzas. It happens, although quite seldom, that she evokes other *Rāmāyaṇa* personages, e.g. when asking two of Daśaratha's sons for their protection. For example, at the end of a few strophes from her *Ayodhyakāṇḍam* we find: "I resort to Bharata along with his younger brother" (*bharataṁ sānujaṁ bhaje*). In this *pāda* the poetess describes Bharata's behaviour after Daśaratha's death. Bharata found consolation in the company of his younger brother Śatrughna and *sānuja* refers to him.

Thus Amba's account of Rāma's exploits, her *Rāmāyaṇastuti*, literally "Praise of Rāma's journey", is not only an epitome, i.e. *sāra*, but also a *stotra*—a hymn eulogising a god or a prayer in a poetical form—as she herself states in many places. In her literary enterprise, Amba not only retells the main events presented in Vālmīki's *Rāmāyaṇa* but also, at the same time, sings the glory of Rāma and asks him for protection. This combination of narrative and prayer parts is the main characteristic of her *magnum opus*.

It is not the only example of such an attitude of an author although there are not many of them. Another such work was composed by Nilakantha Dikshita (Skt. *nīlakaṇṭha dīkṣita*), born in the second half of the 16th century, a minister at the court of Madurai and a versatile scholar and writer. In his *Rāmāyaṇasārasaṃgraha*, also known as *Raghuvīrastava*, consisting of only 33 verses, he praises Rāma and at the same time briefly recapitulates the *Rāmāyaṇa* (Unni 1995: 43). Because of the small volume of his work the poet could only mention major incidents in Rāma's life.[163] In comparison, Amba created a total of 441 stanzas, thus she could provide quite a detailed retelling of the *Rāmāyaṇa* and, simultaneously, with the last quarter of each of them, add a new bead to her rosary or another invocation and supplication to the God in her litany.

Her narration, faithfully and lucidly, without using sophisticated literary means and without her own analysis of the hero's behaviour, guides the reader or listener through the most important events described in *Rāmāyaṇa* as it is in the stanza taken from the *Ayoddhyākaṇḍa*:

vasiṣṭham āhūya mudā narendro
rāmābiṣekasya dinaṁ vicārya /
samārabhat tat bharatasya mātā
nivārayāmāsa hare namas te //3//

Summoning Vasiṣṭha, with joy considering
the day of Rāma's consecration,
the King began (acting in this direction),
what Bharata's mother stopped.
Oh Hari, salutation to you!

Amba also wrote poems to Sarasvatī, the goddess of learning and arts, during the days of the Navaratri[164] festival. Some of these verses are still available, although they were distributed

[163] It is interesting to notice what incidents the poet had chosen. His narration very often seems to contradict the picture of righteous and virtuous Rāma. E.g.:

Rāmāyaṇasārasaṃgraha

tvām eva nātham upayātavator arāteḥ sodaryayoḥ samam avindata rājyam ekaḥ /
anyā tu niṣkaruṇam eva virūpitāsīd īdṛgvidhāni hṛdayāni maheśvarāṇām //19//

Of the brother and sister of the enemy, who equally recognized you as the guardian,
he received the kingdom, she without mercy was disfigured.
These are the hearts of great lords.

[164] In South India Sarasvatī gains a lot of attention during the Navaratri festival days, especially on the tenth and conclusive day.

among Amba's daughters.[165] Her life was very simple, and as it was in ancient, very orthodox, Kshathriya families of Kerala, a saintly one. She died in 2010.

[165] I was promised that the members of the family would try to collect the verses and I would have access to them. Their efforts were fruitful as in 2018 the anthology *Bhaktisagaram* was published containing 30 short poems.

Fig. 15. Sri Dharma Sastha Kshetra of Punjar.

Fig. 16. Madhura Meenakshi Temple of Punjar.

Fig. 17. Madhura Meenakshi Temple of Punjar.

Fig. 18. Kanjiramattam old house, Punjar.

Fig. 19. Karttika Tirunal Amba Tampuratti, mother of Makayiram Nal Amba Tampuratti.

Fig. 20. Putusseri Narayanan Namubudiri, father of Makayiram Nal Amba Tampuratti.

Fig. 21. Makayiram Nal Amba Tampuratti (1917–2010).

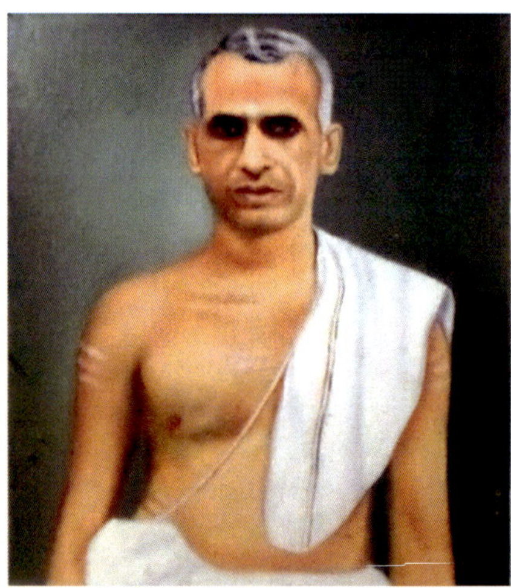

Fig. 22. Kodanad Narayanan Nambudiripad, husband of Makayiram Nal Amba Tampuratti.

Fig. 23. Koyikkal Palace, Punjar.

Fig. 24. Koyikkal compound's wall and the steps leading to the bank of the Meenachil River and the Sastha Temple.

Fig. 25. Kanjiramattam Kottaram, Punjar.

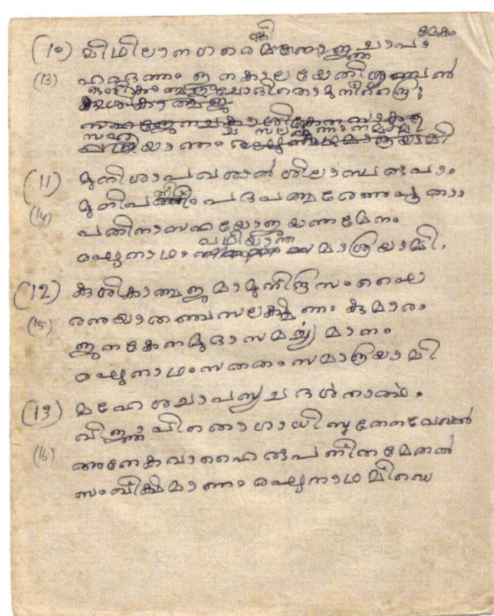

Fig. 26. A page from the *Rāmāyaṇastuti* by Makayiram Nal Amba Tampuratti in her own handwriting.

IV. Three Generations of Women Literati from the Cochin Royal Linage and Their Intellectual Environment

1. The Royal Family of Cochin

The princely state of Cochin with its rulers of Perumpadappu Svarupam came to political prominence at the beginning of the 16th century, although its history is much longer than that. As tradition has it, the Perumpadappu family descends in the maternal line from the Cheras (Sreedhara Menon 2014: 150) (Figs 30–31, p. 133). The city of Makotai was the abode of the Perumpadappus "at least until about 1341 A. D., when they are believed to have transferred the capital to Cochin" (Narayanan 1996: 78). Though small, the state contributed a lot to Sanskrit learning and literature. At the court of the rulers of Cochin literary and intellectual life blossomed. The most important king at the time of the Portuguese settlement, Keshava[166] Rama Varma Tampuran (1565–1601), was a patron of men of letters. The Cochin Royal Family itself has produced outstanding Sanskrit scholars. Vira Kerala Varma (*vīra kēraḷavarma*; reigned 1809–1828), a great patron of learning, composed Sanskrit poems himself and one of his writ-

[166] Skt. *keśava*—an epithet of Viṣṇu-Kṛṣṇa.

ings is the *Pūrṇatrayīśaśataka*—one hundred stanzas dedicated to Pūrṇatrayīśa, who became the dynastic deity of the Cochin Royal Family worshipped in the Trippunitura[167] temple. Rama Varma (1851–1931), known as Rajarishi (Skt. *rājarṣi*), established a Sanskrit *pāṭhaśāla* in Trippunitura for his teacher Śeshacharya (Skt. *śeṣācārya*). The next and last king of Cochin, Rama Varma Parikshit (Skt. *parīkṣit*), in order to promote Sanskrit studies, founded the Sanskrit College in Trippunitura, an institution which still exists and publishes rare Sanskrit manuscripts. Such a background contributed directly to making Ikku Amma Tampuran and her female descendants poetesses.

2. Ikku Amma Tampuran

Subhadra (< Skt. *subhadrā*), known as **Ikku Amma Tampuran** (Fig. 27, p. 113), was born in 1844, in the month of Medam (Mal. *meṭam*, April/May) on the Makayiram asterism, as the daughter of Kunju (Mal. *kuññu*) Nambudiripad of Kudalatupurattu (Mal. *kūṭalāttupurattu*) Mana and Kunjpilla (Mal. *kuññippilla*) Tampuratti of the Cochin Royal Family. She was married to Chennas (Mal. *cennās*) Nambudiripad called Narayanan, who specialized in Vedic rituals. The couple brought up three sons: Rama Varma, Kerala Varma, Ravi Varma and two daughters: Subhadra and Manku (Mal. *maṅku*). Their eldest son, Rama Varma, died prematurely at the age of 23. The sons obtained both traditional Sanskrit education as well as an English one. Kerala Varma was the first prince from the Cochin Royal Family who received B.A. degree. Ravi Varma was a post-graduate and held the post of sub-judge in Madras government service. The two daughters were well-educated in Sanskrit.

Ikku Amma was taught by many Sanskrit scholars. Her early education in Sanskrit was under Mulikkuladu Kunjunni (Mal. *mū-*

[167] Also written down as Tripunithura, Anglicized form < Mal. Tṛppūṇittura/Tṛppūṇattura/Tṛppūṇattara.

Fig. 27. Subhadra Tampuratti of the Royal Family of Cochin (1844–1921).

likkulaṭu kuññuṇṇi) Nambyar;[168] then dramas (Skt. *nāṭaka*) and poetics (Skt. *alaṃkāraśāstra*) under Palapurattu Pudiyetadu (Mal. *pālappurattu putiyeṭatu*) Govindan Nambiyar; *tarka* or logic under Patudol (Mal. *paṭutol*) Vidvan (Skt. *vidvān*) Nambudiripad and *vyākaraṇa* or grammar under Subrahmanyan Edappalam (Mal. *subrahmaṇyan eṭappalam*) Nambudiri (Kunjunni Raja 1980: 261). In her own compositions she mentions Edappalam Nambudiri as her guru. As her great granddaughter Chandravali Tampuran put it, she was a personality of harmonious blending of *bhakti-jñāna-vairagya*, namely devotion, knowledge and non-attachment to worldly things.[169] She was filled with a great passion for knowledge. Every day she would read *purāṇas* and *upaniṣads*. She maintained regular contact with Sanskrit scholars and studied various works all her life. In order to be in touch with the Kodun-

[168] Mal. *nampiyār*—1. a subcaste of the Ambalavasi (Mal. *ampalavāsi*) community, 2. a title bestowed by a king, 3. an official in a temple (after Schildt 2012: 211).

[169] From the notes prepared by Chandravali Tampuran.

gallur circle of literati and scholars, she stayed in Tiruvanchikulam (Mal. *tiruvañcikkulam*),[170] which is close to Kodungallur. The intellectually stimulating atmosphere of the Veṇmaṇi movement,[171] which she was able to share, together with her thorough Sanskrit education and the talents she possessed enabled her to write many compositions both in Sanskrit and Malayalam.

One of her works was the *Saubhadrastavam*, consisting of 41 verses in which she summarised the message of the *Śrīmadbhāgavatam* and another eight stanzas drawing on the *Devīmāhātmyam*. She also wrote Sanskrit *stotras*, or hymns, such as the one in ten verses which she prays to be in her mind at the time of her death and containing the description of god Pūrṇatrayīśa from head to toe, i.e. the *Pūrṇatrayīśakeśādipāda-varṇanam*, or other ones, such as the *Bhagavatyaṣṭaka*, *Śivakeśādipādavarṇaṇam*, *Bhagavatīkeśādipādavarṇanam*, *Vañculeśastava* and *Purāṇālayādhīśvarīstotra*.

One more hymn dedicated to Pūrṇatrayīśa is known as the *Pūrṇatrayīśastotram*. It consists of 46 stanzas and almost all of them refer to Viṣṇu's incarnations. Out of them as many as seven stanzas, starting from 20 to 26, describe the acts of Rāma, and fourteen couplets (28 to 41) present the history of Kṛṣṇa. Major events are emphasized, and let strophe 24, referring to Rāma, serve as an example:

> *hatvā laṅkādhipaṃ yaḥ sutasahajabhaṭāmātyayuktaṃ ca yuddhe*
> *sītāmādāya pūtāṃ jvalanapatanataḥ puṣpakaṃ cādhiruhya /*
> *rājyaṃ gatvā ca pūjyair munibhir atha kṛtasvābhiṣekaḥ svakīyaiḥ*
> *sārdhaṃ tatrāvasas tvaṃ janam anuramayan pāhi pūrṇatrayīśa!* //24//[172]

[170] In Tiruvanchikulam there is a famous Mahādeva temple, which was associated first with the Cheras, then with the Perumpadappu Svarupam. It is one of the oldest Śiva temples in South India. It is connected with the Chidambaram temple in Tamil Nadu. Śiva of Tiruvanchikulam is the dynastic deity of the Cochin Royal Family.

[171] More about this literary movement in George 1968: 139–142.

[172] Subhadra 1965: 6.

You,
who in the battle annihilated the master of Laṅkā,
having his brother as minister and sons for warriors,
you took Sītā, purified after entering the fire.
And having got on the Puṣpaka chariot,
you returned to the country.
The most wonderful sages along with
your people placed you on the throne.
And you settled there, loving the subjects.
Protect us, oh Pūrṇatrayīśa!

Far less space was devoted to the remaining incarnations, even Rāma with Axe (Paraśurāma), the mythological creator of Kerala, is recalled in one strophe only:

jāto yo reṇukāyāṃ mudam atha jamadagneśca mātuś ca kurvan
dattātreyāttavidyākṛtamadakṛtavīryātmajādīn narendrān /
niśśeṣaṃ nāśayitvā bhuvamatha vigatakṣatriyāṃ cāpi kṛtvā
cāddhāraṃ keralānāṃ prasabhamakuruthāḥ pāhi pūrṇatrayīśa! //27//

Born from Reṇukā, you
certainly pleased Jamadagni and the mother.
Annihilating the conceited son of Kṛtavīrya,
who received the knowledge from Dattātreya,
You destroyed the entire earth
And brought the death to *kṣatriyas*.
And the land of Kerala you tore out violently.
Protect us, Pūrṇatrayīśa!

The poetess directly addresses the heroes of her stanzas, finishing each of them with the incantation: "Protect (us), oh Pūrṇatrayīśa!" (*pāhi pūrṇatrayīśa*).[173]

She also composed some *kīrtans*, mainly in Manipravalam.

Ikku Amma also taught Sanskrit to the members of her family. Even teaching the *Siddharūpam* to the children was a pleasure for

[173] This phrase has been chosen by her great-granddaughter Chandravali Tampuran as the title of the anthology containing the hymns in Sanskrit and Malayalam mainly written by Kerala women.

her. Among her pupils was her younger cousin, the future king Rama Varma, known as Rajarishi Tampuran.[174]

Her great-granddaughter Chandravali Tampuran recalls the stories repeated by the family members and picturing Ikku Amma as a very strong personality, able to impose her will. As a very young girl she was betrothed to one man but she married another, whom she found more suitable. Nobody could question her about that. She was also bold enough to object the family tradition as to the selection of her children's names. According to the family customs the names for boys and girls were determined by the sequence of their birth. The name of a first son should be Rama Varma, the second one should be named Kerala Varma and the third Ravi Varma. For the girls the set of particular names was also established: Amba and Subhadra. However, after her third son passed away she decided to name the fourth one again Ravi Varma. Also for her daughters she selected the names against the normally accepted habit. Her first daughter was called after her mother Subhadra and the second one Manku.

She died in 1921, in the month of Minam (Mal. *mīnam*; March/April), on the Ayiliyam asterism.[175]

3. Manku Tampuran and her descendants

Her daughter, **Manku Tampuran** (Fig. 28, p. 117), born in 1884, in the month of Tulam (Mal. *tulām*, October/November) on the

---

[174] He, although a patron of the poets and scholarly life, authored himself only one work which was published, namely the *Vedāntaparibhāṣasaṃgraha*. His life was described by different Sanskrit poets, e.g. in the *mahākāvya* in ten cantos entitled *Śrīrāmavijaya* by Kunjan Variyar (Mal. kuññan vāriyar) (Kunjunni Raja 1980: 267).

[175] My Polish translations of fragments from her *Pūrṇatrayīśastotram* were published in *Przegląd Orientalistyczny* 1–2, 2016, in the article devoted to the three generations of the poetesses from the Royal Family of Cochin (Sudyka 2016).

Visakham star, following her mother, started to compose poems. She was married to Sankaran Nambudiripad of Kudalattuparatu Mana (Mal. *śaṅkaran kūṭalāttupuratu mana*) and the couple had four daughters: Rameshvari (Mal. *rāmeśvari*), Kunjipillakutti (Mal. *kuññippillakuṭṭi*), Ikkutti (Mal. *ikkuṭṭi*) and Kochchammini (Mal. *koccāmmini*) and one son—Rama Varma Kunjunni.

Fig. 28. Manku Tampuran of the Royal Family of Cochin (1884–1977).

Manku Tampuran was devoted to the analysis of different religious Sanskrit texts, sometimes using Telugu sources in order to understand better the meaning of the text under study. She composed many shorter and longer poems. Some of them are collected in the booklet edited in 1964 in Trippunitura, entitled *Stutiratnamālā* or "The Jewel Garland of Hymns". The collection is dedicated to the memory of her mother. This is a two-stanza poem *Mātṛsmaraṇam*:

ahaṃ pramūḍhāpi madīyamātā
prājñā praśastaprathitā subhadrā /
nāmni pramagnā nigameśabhaktā
nityaṃ purāṇaśravaṇe prasaktā //

śāstrapravīṇā kavitārasajñā
kāmye viraktā karuṇārdracitā /
tatsambhavatvād aham alpam adya
pravaktum īśe tadanugraheṇa //[176]

I am dull-witted.
My mother, called Subhadrā, was intelligent, praised widely,
immersed in and worshipping the Lord of the Vedas,
devoted constantly to the *purāṇa* studies,
versed in *śāstras*, knowing the taste of poetry,
indifferent to (her own) desires, with a heart tender out of compassion.
Because of the closeness with her and her favour,
I possess this little amount (of knowledge) to speak (i.e. compose).

These two stanzas are quite a rare example of autobiographical mentions in Sanskrit writings. It seems that we detect two levels of reference. First, there is the relation between a mother and her highly respectful daughter. Manku puts herself in the shadow of her famous, knowledgeable and talented poetess mother. She does not want to compete with her, just admire her skills and commemorate her vast knowledge as well as indomitable spirit. On the other hand, in the background, these two stanzas could be regarded as following Sanskrit literary convention of praising one's teachers[177] and model poets and depreciating one's own poetic skills.[178] Probably both these attitudes are valid. In this short two-stanza-long poem, Manku gives some personal information confirming what we know about her mother's education and her practice of daily studies. It is also significant that the *Mātṛsmaraṇam* acts as the dedication-poem, placed on a separate page at the beginning of the booklet.[179] What is also worth

[176] Manku: 1964.

[177] Ikku Amma used to teach Sanskrit to the children of the family, as was mentioned above.

[178] It could work as *captatio benevolentiae*, a rhetorical technique practiced by Roman orators.

[179] On the opposite page there is another dedication entitled *Samarpaṇam*—

noticing is the fact that, in spite of the very traditional title, the *Stutiratnamālā* no longer shares the traditional pattern of ancient manuscripts. It can be placed within the modern print culture overlaying the collection of traditional short poems such as *stotras* or *stavas*, eight-stanza-long hymns (Skt. *aṣṭaka*) and the descriptions of gods from head to foot. It combines the traditional contents with a modern layout. Besides the dedication-poem mentioned above, there is a list of contents—in Sanskrit *viṣayāḥ*—with the names of all the hymns; the errors (*aśuddham*) and their corrections (*śuddham*) are enumerated at the end; we find the place of publication on the front page, in both the Anglicized version, Tripunithura, and also in the Sanskritized one—Pūrṇavedapurī;[180] and the name of the publisher is given—Raja Press—also rendered in Sanskrit as *rājā prasū* (Fig. 29, p. 120). At that point it is worth remembering the last king of Cochin, Rama Varma Parikshit, who founded the still-existing Sanskrit College in Trippunitura in order to promote Sanskrit studies. The institution used to publish rare Sanskrit manuscripts and perhaps from the same printing press Manku's small anthology of poems comes. Perhaps the Raja Press looked exactly like the abovemen-

the apostrophe to Viṣṇu, in which she equates the attitude of a trusting child to the mother with the relations of the worshiper and god, who kindly looks even at imperfect human works:

mayā proktam idaṃ stotraṃ
saguṇaṃ vāpi nirguṇam /
tvayy arpaye hare sarvaṃ
yathā bālaḥ svamātari //

This hymn composed by me,
has some qualities or lacks them.
All I offer to You, Hari,
like a child to his mother.

[180] There is an etiological myth explaining the name of Trippunitura as originating from Pūrṇavedapurī. According to legend, a Brahmins' village was situated there, which resounded with Vedic hymns and emanated the atmosphere of holiness (Vaidyanathan 1982: 210).

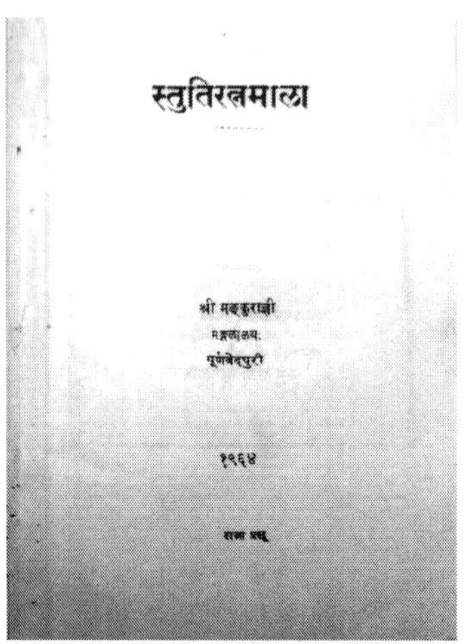
स्तुतिरत्नमाला

१९६४

Fig. 29. *Stutiratnamālā* of Manku, the title page.

tioned Narendra Printers at Mannadiar Lane in Trissur (Fig. 6, p. 84).

The *Stutiratnamālā* consists of 11 hymns and prayers to different gods; nevertheless, the main portion of them express *bhakti* to Pūrṇatrayīśa, a fact that reflects Manku's ardent devotion to this particular god.

In the hymn *Prārthanā* containing 44 stanzas she worships Pūrṇatrayīśa:

pūrṇatrayīśa tava pādasarojayugmaṃ
pūrṇapramodam aniśaṃ hṛdi cintayāmi /
arṇojapatrasamanetra kṛpālavasya
tūrṇaṃ bhajāni tava bhājanatāṃ dayābdhe //2//[181]

Oh Pūrṇatrayīśa!
Constantly, with immeasurable joy,
I contemplate your lotus feet in my heart.
You, with eyes like lotus petals on the water!

[181] Manku 1964: 9.

Ocean of compassion!
I am quickly heading towards
the treasury of particles of your pity.

In stanzas addressed to her beloved god Manku employs similes and other poetic devices passed down for hundreds of years within classical Sanskrit poetry (*kāvya*):

indīvarākṣaṃ śaradinduvaktraṃ
bimbādharoṣṭhaṃ sitakundadantam /
mandāramālādivirājitaṃ tvāṃ
vande mukundaṃ munivṛndavandyam //26//

I adore you, Mukunda, with eyes like blue water lilies and
a face like an autumnal moon, with a *bimba*-like mouth
and white teeth like jasmine flowers,
shining because of *mandāra* garlands
and other (decorations) -
worthy to be adored by hosts of sages.

These conventional similes: teeth compared to the flowers of jasmine *kunda* (*Jasminum multiflorum*), lips, or actually the lower lip, to the red *bimba* (*Momordica monadelpha*), face to the shining moon, belonged to the stylistic devices that a good poet skillfully used in a new configuration, creating aesthetic qualities admired by the recipients. The poetess employs comparisons generally used to describe the beauty of a woman and with their help she created the image of a god—a colourful picture that radiates shine.

She took care of sound instrumentation of the stanzas, using alliterations (Skt. *anuprāsa*) and *yamakas*,[182] which certainly

[182] Skt. *yamaka*—the stylistic figure is built in such a way that part of the stanza repeats according to a specific pattern; most Sanskrit treatises on poetic stress that the meaning of repetitive elements must be different, which was achieved by setting different morpheme boundaries. This figure of sound was particularly popular among poets of Kerala. Some of them were called the "poets of *yamaka*", like for instance Vasudeva (15th century) of the famous Payyur Bhatta (Mal. *payyūr bhaṭṭa*) family was addressed as Vāsudevayamakakavi (Skt., Mal.).

icreased the value of her poetry. These stylistic measures were appreciated as increasing the musicality of the poem, after all, intended to be listened to and have its sounds enjoyed. Take stanza 15 of the "Prayer" or *Prāthanā* as an example:

nigamanilayavāso nirmalāpītavāso
nirupamamṛduhāso nirmamāntarnivāsaḥ /
nikhilabhuvanavāso niścalapremadāso
mama hṛdayanivāsas syās sadā śrīnivāsaḥ //15//

In addition to alliterations, we also have a *yamaka* outlined here—*vāsa* can mean dress, clothes, or clothing. So *nirmalāpītavāsa* means "one who has yellowish shinning garment" and *śrīnivāsa*, the Vishnu epithet, means "abode (*nivāsa*) of the goddess Śrī".

The titles of her other devotional hymns, for example, *Pūrṇatrayīśasuprabhātam* and *Pūrṇatrayīśastotram*, also indicate her particular devotion to the god residing in the Trippunitura temple, a fact that was already visible in the *Stutiratnamālā*. The *Pūrṇatrayīśasuprabhātam* belongs to the genre of hymns sung to the god in the morning.[183] Just like the bards used to wake up the king at his court, the waking up ceremony of the god takes place in the temple.[184]

Besides the poems gathered in *The Jewel Garland of Hymns* and those in the *Pāhi Pūrṇatrayīśa!*, she wrote the *Santānagopālam* in 30 verses.[185]

It turns out that the *Santānagopālam* is linked tightly with the Pūrṇatrayīśa temple (Figs 32–35, p. 134–135) legend and perhaps with Manku's life, too. The plot is known from the *Bhāgavatapurāṇa* 10.86 (K. K. Shastree 1997: 300–307). It goes as fol-

[183] Skt. *suprabhāta*, literally a beautiful dawn or day break.

[184] In the south of India perhaps the most well-known morning prayers and ceremony of waking up the god takes place in Veṅkateśvara Temple in Tirupati.

[185] The poem was published but I was not able to trace the collection in which it appeared. The copy in my possession comes from Chandravali Tampuran's private archives. The whole text is provided in the Appendix.

lows: after the Kurukshetra battle, when Arjuna visits Kṛṣṇa in Dvaraka[186] he meets a Brahmin, all of whose children died at birth, lamenting over his fate. Arjuna sympathizes with the Brahmin and promises him that he will not lose any child his wife may bear in the future. Arjuna makes a vow that if he fails to protect the Brahmin's child, he will immolate himself. Soon the Brahmin's wife is expecting again. Before the delivery day Arjuna goes to the Brahmin's house to make certain that the god of death will not be able to snatch the newborn away. Unfortunately, this time the Brahmin's child miraculously disappears. Arjuna looks for the baby everywhere but in vain. When he prepares to enter the fire, Kṛṣṇa arrives and informs him that he knows the whereabouts of all the Bharmin's children. Kṛṣṇa and Arjuna, together, embark on a journey through the worlds. On their way they cross seven regions of terrestrial world (*dvīpa*) and seven oceans, then the region of darkness, beyond which the supreme light shines. While the divine chariot is crossing the region of light, it enters the region of water. There they meet Viṣṇu, reposing on the coils of the huge snake Ādiśeṣa. They learn from the God that the Brahmin's children are there and that the reason for taking them from their parents was to bring both Kṛṣṇa and Arjuna before him in order to show their virtues and in this way set an example for people. Kṛṣṇa and Arjuna return to Dvaraka with the Brahmin's sons and give them back to their delighted parents. And this is the end of the story as told in the *Bhāgavata*. However, on Kerala's soil, in a particular place on the map, it is continued. Arjuna was given an idol—Santānagopālamūrti, for which he wanted to find the best place on the earth. He was accompanied by Gaṇeśa in his search, and, as some versions of the legend proclaim, it was Gaṇeśa who first found the village where the Brahmins lived. It was called Pūrṇavedapuram and resounded with Vedic hymns and emanated the atmosphere of holiness. Gaṇeśa decided to take this place over

[186] Skt. *dvārakā*—the capital city of Kṛṣṇa's clan.

for himself, however, Arjuna did not let him do that and established Santānagopālamūrti there. Then a temple was built there, which was named Pūrṇatrayīśa, i.e. the temple of the Lord of Three *Vedas* (*Ṛgveda*, *Yajurveda* and *Sāmaveda*). The place is nowadays a suburb of Kochi and is called Trippunitura. Known as the Poornatrayeesa Temple, it is visited by many a childless couple, as it is believed to be the best place to ask the God for a child. Certainly, plenty of stories circulate about childless couples blessed by the God after worshipping the Viṣṇu-Kṛṣṇa idol—Santānagopālamūrti (the idol of the Protector of Progeny)—which is placed there. The popularity of the place and the special interest people of Kerala take in this Puranic story may be accounted for by the beliefs that this is the place where its protagonists appeared in person; as legend has it, not only the gods, but also the Brahmin from Dvaraka moved to Pūrṇavedapuram and became the chief priest in the temple. Nambudiris from Puliyanur (Mal. *puliyanūr*) are said to be the descendants of that Brahmin (Vaidyanathan 1982: 210).

However, this is not the only temple in Kerala where one can pray before Santānagopāla, there are some more. One of them is the quite famous shrine near Changanacherry. It is said to have been built by Rani Gouri Lakshmi Bayi and her husband Rajaraja Varma Koyil Tampuran of the Lakshmipuram Palace. They had no male children and thus the survival of Travancore was at stake because for the lack of heir to the throne the British Empire could annex the kingdom. To beget a male child they decided to have a shrine built and one year after its completion the Queen became pregnant with future monarch Svati Tirunal Rama Varma, who, although still in his mother's womb, was proclaimed the successor of the Travancore throne. Another Santānagopāla temple is Petṛkōvil, Cittārikāvu (Mal.) (Figs 36–37, p. 136). It is a charming, calm place situated among Keralan green fields and groves, not very far from Calicut.[187]

---

[187] Thanks to Dr. Geethakumary (Calicut University) and Mr. Rajesh K., a

One can wonder why the story from the *Bhāgavatapurāṇa* with its many versions has gained so much popularity. It is believed that besides prayers offered to the God, also each and every recapitulation of its plot acts in the same way—not only can it bring the progeny but also help in protecting them. That is why so many authors have used the story as canvas to create their own narratives.

There is a great number of works based on the Santānagopāla theme.[188] One of them is a Sanskrit poem *Santānagopālam* ascribed to the famous Narayana Bhatta of Melpputtur. Puntanam (Mal. *pūntānam*) Nambudiri, Narayana Bhatta's friend, is the author of the *Santānagopālacampū* in the Malayalam language. Another *Santānagopālacampū*, this time in Sanskrit, was written by the ruler of Travancore Asvati Tirunal Rama Varma (1755–1795). It was edited and published, with its Malayalam translation, by C. Unnikrishna Varriyar (Kunjunni Raja 1980: 173) and there is also another edition, this time with extensive and highly interesting commentary by P. Govindaru Nambudirippad, published in 1954. But that theme is also covered in anonymous works, e.g. *Santānagopālaprabandha*. In Kerala literary tradition *prabandha*s were compositions based on Puranic lore and presented as the so-called *kūttu* on the stage by a *cākyār*, a professional actor of Sanskrit plays. With regards to Kerala performing arts we can also notice the Kathakali tradition using the story from the *Bhāgavata* (Zarilli 1994). Another anonymous composition represents *laghukāvya*, i.e. a short poem. It is the *Santānagopālam* of only seven stanzas (Easwaran Nampoothiry 1972: 153). According to Kunjunni Raja, Ambadi (Mal. ambāḍi) Devaki Amma "has recently produced a musical Radio play, *Santānagopāla*" (Kunjunni Raja 1980: 274). When such a theme of obtaining and pro-

Ph.D. candidate (Calicut University), I was able to reach this temple.

[188] The works in Sanskrit are mentioned in Kunjunni Raja 1980: 238, 135, 146, 173f, 271, 268f, 274.

tecting progeny was exploited by women writers, were they just relating the Puranic story or unveiling some details from their own life? After all, bearing children and taking care of them were the dominating concerns in their lives. How then was it in Manku Tampuran's case?

What we know is that Manku had no children for the first three years of her married life. After her pilgrimage to Rameshvaram[189] in Tamil Nadu, she gave birth to her first daughter and gave her a meaningful name—Rameshvari.[190]

Her poem relating the story from the *Bhāgavatapurāṇa* can be treated as closely connected with her own life, even if the text of this little poem authored by her is silent about her longing for a child. Usually we know very little about the lives of authoresses but it seems that one should not consider the selection of such a theme as accidental. In the last stanza, suddenly abandoning the plot of the Puranic story, she connects it not with her own life but with the Trippunitura temple so well known to her:

> *phalguno hariṇā dattaṃ bimbam ādāya sādaram /*
> *pūrṇatrayīśapure sthāpya paraṃ harṣam avāptavān //30//*
>
> Arjuna, after respectfully taking the image offered by Hari and establishing it in the Pūrṇatrayīśa City, was overjoyed.

Manku also wrote in Manipravalam and Malayalam,[191] again taking spiritual matters as the subject of her writings. Her works *Kāśiyātra* and *Badariyātra*, the travelogues in Malayalam verse, were and still are a kind of a guidebook for those Keralites who undertake a pilgrimage to these places.

---

[189] Skt. *rāmeśvaram*—one of the holiest places in India, with the famous Śiva temple visited by many pilgrimes.

[190] From the notes prepared by her granddaughter Chandravali Tampuran.

[191] The anthology *Pahi Pūrṇatrayīśa!* edited by Chandravali Tampuran contains a Sanskrit hymn by Manku entitled *Śrīpūrṇatrayīśasuprabhātam*, as well as seven peans in Malayalam.

Manku Tampuran supervised the Sanskrit education of her children but did not teach them herself. Whenever the teachers came, she was present listening to the lessons.

The reminiscence of her graceful personality is still with her granddaughter Chandravali, whom I met in February 2015. She remembers Sanskrit scholars coming to their house and discussing poems and problems concerning literary creation. Chandravali was quite often asked to rewrite the poems as her handwriting was considered very elegant. Chandravali Tampuran stresses that her grandmother had very defined objectives and a marked-out way of life but she understood that the way of life changes.

She died in 1977, in the month of Dhanu (December/January) on the Ayiliyam star.

Ikku Amma Tampuran and Manku Tampuran, mother and her daughter, lived a very religious life centred around the temple and mirrored in their literary creativity. All their works can be labelled as religious writings. Among their works one can find *stutis* or hymns to gods and pieces based on Puranic lore. They wrote with only one thought in mind: to express their devotion to gods, not seeking fame and popularity. Their way of life was very simple with no distractions at all. Their days, one similar to another, were marked only by temple festivals or pilgrimages.

Koccāmmini (Mal.) **Tampuran**, the daughter of Manku Thampuran, born in 1913, in the month of Midhunam (Mal. *mithunam*, June/July) on the Choti star, also received a good Sanskrit education but she had formal school education too and obtained her Secondary School Leaving Certificate. She was married to Sankaran Nambudiripad of Kilottukara (Mal. *kīḻottukāra*) Mana and they had four children: two sons—Ramabhadran (Mal. *rāmabhadran*) and Srikumaran (Mal. *śrīkumāran*), and two daughters—Nandaja and Subhadra. She passed away in 1985, in the month of Vrischikam (Mal. *vṛścikam*, November/December) on the Utram star.

She wrote only a few poems in Sanskrit and Malayalam. Two Sanskrit and two Malayalam hymns were published in the collection *Pāhi Pūrṇatrayīśa!*.

The title of the first composition in Sanskrit, *Pūrṇatrayīśa mama dehi karāvalamba*, comes from the refrain finishing each of 24 verses. It is an invocation with all the stanzas containing epithets of Rāma in vocative forms, but it is Pūrṇatrayīśa who is asked in each verse for help:

> *śrirāmacandra raghupuṅgava rāvaṇāre*
> *śrirāmabhadra bharatāgraja rākṣāre*
> *kodaṇḍarāma bhuvaneśvara viśvakanda*
> *pūrṇatrayīśa mama dehi karāvalamba* //2//[192]
>
> Oh Rāmacandra,[193]
> oh Hero of Raghu's Race, oh Enemy of Rāvaṇa,
> oh Gracious Rāma, Elder Brother of Bharata,
> oh Enemy of Demons, oh Rāma with a Bow,
> oh Lord of the World, the Root of Everything!
> Oh Pūrṇatrayīśa, give me a helping hand!

It seems that the same form presents the second Sanskrit poem of Kochchammini in that collection under the title *Vande devam jagadgurum*. Its stanzas also finish with words used for its title.

> *rāmaṃ rākṣahantāraṃ rāmacandraṃ mahāprabhuṃ* /
> *sītapatiṃ rāvaṇāriṃ vande devaṃ jagadgurum* //1//
>
> I worship Rāma—the Killer of Demons,
> I worship Rāmacandra—the Mighty Lord,
> I worship the Husband of Sītā—the Enemy of Rāvaṇa.
> I worship God—the Father of the World.

This composition, however, contains the account of Rāma's life. Each of 22 stanzas, which come next, points to a certain episode known from Vālmīki's *Rāmāyaṇa*:

---

[192] Chandravali Tampuran (ed.) 2009: 214.

[193] This epithet of Rāma equates him with the moon.

atha sarvaguṇopetā sītā janakanandinī /
yaṃ cakre ramaṇaṃ tuṣṭā vande devam jagadguruṃ //7//

I worship God—the Father of the World,
whom happy Sītā, abounding in all qualities,
daughter of Janaka, made her husband.

citrakūṭe vasan rāmaḥ dṛṣṭva bharatam āśrame /
yo 'dadāt pādukam tasmai vande devam jagadgurum //

Rāma, who was staying in hermitage at Citrakuṭa,
seeing Bharata, gave him his own shoes.
I worship God—the Father of the World.

The purpose of this short poem is therefore similar to the one Amba Tampuratti of Punjar set for herself.

4. Women writers of the Tottakkad Family

After three generations of women literati belonging to the Cochin Royal Family, the names of women close to that court should be mentioned. **Ikkavamma** (Mal. *ikkāvāmma*) of Tottakad (Mal. *toṭṭakāṭ*) belonged to an aristocratic Nayar family, her husband served as a Divan Peshkar[194] for the Cochin Raja. Her father was Irinjalakkuda[195] Nandikkara Panikkar[196]. She was taught not only *kāvya* but also astronomy and astrology. The fact that she studied

[194] Diwan Peshkar was in charge of the police and magisterial wings of the administration.

[195] Mal. *iriññālakkuṭa*—a town in the Trissur district famous for its temple and associated with different Kerala legends.

[196] Mal. *paṇikkar*—besides being a title of a fencing master as well as a honorific title of different castes (e.g. some ministers of Zamorin), it refers to a workman, artisan, especially a master builder (Schildt 2012: 212).

the *Naiṣadhacaritam* proves that her Sanskrit education was at an advanced level. Her only extant works are in Malayalam. Her drama, the *Subhadrārjunam* in Malayalam, was translated into Sanskrit by Kesava Sastri of Karamana in Trivandrum (Kunjunni Raja 1980: 273).

Her daughter Tottakad **Madhavi Amma** (Mal. *mādhavi*, Skt. *mādhavī*) (1888–1968) gained proficiency in Sanskrit, English and other European languages and was a well-known poet and literary critic. She was a member of the Ernakulam Women's Association and

> (...) was nominated an unofficial member to the Cochin Legislative Council in 1925. She was the president of the Women's Conference held as part of the Nair Conference at Karuvatta in 1929.
> (*Devika 2005: 93*)

5. Summing-up

The pictures of these three women, including the fourth generation, Chandrawali Tampuran, show the changes that were made in the way of women's education in Kerala in the 19th and 20th centuries. Ikku Amma enjoyed the reputation of a great Sanskrit scholar. She constantly expanded the traditional education she obtained at home. She created many poems that circulated more widely than her family circle since she had many students. These pieces were probably learnt by heart and recited from memory but only some of them have been preserved. Her daughter Manku was her mother's student and she followed in her footsteps. Although she enjoyed less fame and her works were less known outside her family, her Sanskrit literary legacy has largely survived. In 1964 a collection of her poems was published. It can be said that the printed matter fulfilled its task, however, in the climate of Kerala the existance of such a booklet is very limited in time. In addition, it was available only locally and there are no copies of it in libraries. The *Santānagopāla* poem has also survived, though very few people have heard about it. Another writer in this family did not even develop her wings. Kochchammini received formal secondary education besides the traditional one, successfully passing her final exams. Her education, therefore, went along the path that the new times set. Modern forms of teaching developed from around 1860, especially in the kingdom of Travancore. It was favoured by the politics of the Maharaja of Travancore and supported by the work of Christian missionaries. The new type of education turned out to be useful, widely available for different groups of society and thus became attractive and desirable.[197] Traditional Sanskrit education did not disappear, but was limited. In the new epoch, it was impractical to devote someone's time to studying and continually improving Sanskrit in order to create literature which would not have many recipients, because only those who knew Sanskrit and Sanskrit literature could appreciate it. This is the case of Kochchammini Tampuran. Probably the Western model of education was the reason why she could not focus on composing in Sanskrit, although her knowledge of Sanskrit was good, which she proved by writing small poems.

However, the changes continued on the socio-economic and political level: the social reforms in Kerala, the loss of control over large land properties, the 1912 Nayar Act[198] interfering with the customs of matrilineal families, and finally the disappearance of the kingdoms and principalities and their incorporation into the Republic of India.

The example, again of a mother and her daughter, namely Tottakad Ikkavamma and Madhavi Amma, shows that the modern

[197] More about education in 19th-century Kerala in Jeffrey 1992; Tharakan 1984: 1959–1967.

[198] See for example Jeffrey 1994.

type of education could open the way to quite a spectacular career.

Sanskrit was not necessary to develop it but the knowledge of English could help a lot. As far as literary creation is concerned, besides writers and literary critics still locating themselves within Sanskrit poetics, there was a group who believed that only a turn towards science, materialism and European modernity could finish the servitude of Malayalam to Sanskrit as well as to English sources.[199]

[199] Among such critics was Kesari A. Balakrishna Pillai (Devika 2013: 90–91).

Fig. 30. The entrance to the Amma Tampuran Kovilakam, the ancestral home of the Cochin Royal Family in Trippunitura.

Fig. 31. Amma Tampuran Kovilakam, the ancestral home of the Cochin Royal Family in Trippunitura.

Fig. 32. The courtyard of the Poornatrayeesa Temple, Trippunitura.

Fig. 33. Poornatrayeesa Temple, Trippunitura during festival days. The royal balcony in the background.

Fig. 34. Poornatrayeesa Temple, Trippunitura during festival days. The procession of elephants.

Fig. 35. Poornatrayeesa Temple, Trippunitura during festival days. A percussion ensamble (panchari melam).

Fig. 36. Santanagopala Temple—Petrikovil, Cittarikavu.

Fig. 37. Santanagopala Temple—Petrikovil, Cittarikavu.

V. To the North of Kerala. Lakshmi of the Kadattanad Royal House

In the India Office Library there is a manuscript No. 8158 containing the *Santānagopālakāvya*. The poem was written, as announced in it, by Lakṣmī Rājñī (Skt.). Who was this queen? It seems that little information can be provided. All we know, it seems, is that she was born in 1845 and died in 1909, and that she belonged to the Kadattanad Royal Family.

1. History of Kadattanad

Kadattanad was a small principality in the northern part of Malabar. The famous folk songs *Vadakkaṅ Pāṭṭukaḷ* or "Northern Ballads" show some heroes and heroines living there in medieval times (Mathew 1979: 8).[200] The territory of this coastal realm was stretched between the Kotta River (Mal. *kōṭṭa*) in the south and the present Mahé[201] in the north, i.e. in the modern Vadakara (Mal. *vaṭakara*) taluk, the Calicut district. Due to such geographical position the small kingdom had to negotiate its political standing with its neighbours and all the newcomers to the region

[200] The *Northern Ballads* can be dated back to the 15th century CE at the earliest.

[201] Mal. *māhe*, a small town and the name of the district as well as the name of a river; a part of French India.

all the time. The sea opened the door to trade and fishery but it could also bring invaders.

The origins of that kingdom are connected with the Polanad (Mal. *pōlanāṭ˘*) rulers, i.e. Polatiris/Poralatiris (Mal. *polātiri*/*poralāttiri*). The *Kēraḷolpatti* (Mal. < Mal. *kēraḷa* + Skt. *utpatti*—origin, birth), the traditional history of Kerala,[202] while giving the account of the partition of the Chera kingdom into 17 smaller and bigger principalities, names Polanad among seven major ones, with 10 000 *nāyar*s and 72 *tara*s (*nāyar* villages), 5 *akampati*s (companions) and a residence in the Mallūr (Mal.) palace (Naryanan 2003: 67). As it was so close to the expansive power of the ruler of Eranad, who later acquired the title of Zamorin and ruled from Calicut, it was only a matter of time before fighting started. After years of continuous struggles with their powerful enemies, the Polatiris somewhat mysteriously disappeared from the scene only to reappear centuries later. One finds descendants of a Polatiri lady settled near Vadakara and its surrounding area, where they ruled with the permission granted by the Kolattiris (Mal. *kōlattiri*). The name Kolattiri denotes the Chirakkal (Mal. *ciṟakkal̲*) rulers, whose country was known as Kolattunad (Mal. *kōlattunāṭu˘*).[203] It is said that the Polatiri princess married a Kolattiri prince and in that way originated the dynasty which ruled Kadattanad territories, named like this because one had to 'cross'[204] this land on the way from the Zamorin's kingdom to that of the Kolattiris and the other way round (Sreedhara Menon 2014: 171–172). They ruled as the vassals of the Kolattiris titled *vaḻḻunnavar*s (Mal.) and only in 1750 they assumed the title of

[202] The *Kēraḷolpatti* is a Malayalam counterpart of Sanskrit *Keralamahātmyam*. There were many versions of the "Origin of Kerala", with alternations introduced in order to please the local patrons. Possibly, the original is older than the 16th century (Narayanan 2003: 192).

[203] About the Kolattunad and Kolattiris read in Mailaparambil 2012.

[204] The Malayalam verb *kaṭatt* means "to ford", "to ferry".

rāja. Besides the Kuttippuram (Mal. *kuṭṭippuṟam*) Kovilakam, two other branches of the family were established: the Onchiyam (Mal. *oñciyam*) Kovilakam and the Purameri (Mal. *puṟamēri*) Kovilakam.[205] In 1703 Alexander Hamilton visited Burgara, as he transliterates the name of Vadakara, later on anglicized as Badagara. He described the kingdom and its ruler in such words:

> And eight or ten Miles farther to the Southward, is Burgara, a Seaport in the Dominions of Ballanore Burgarie, a formidable prince. His Country produces Pepper, and the best Cardamums in the World. I once called at his Port, and bought 40 Tuns of Cardamums for the Surat Market.
> (*Hamilton 1995 II: 298–299*)[206]

The word Ballanore must be a corrupted form of *vaḷḷunnavar*, i.e. a chieftain. The name of the ruler is not given by Hamilton but according to family tradition its male members were named Sankaravarman, Manavarman, Ravivarman, Udayavarman or Krishnavarman. The ladies of the ruling family could assume any of the following six names: Lakshmi, Madhavi, Parvati, Sridevi (Mal. *śrīdēvi*) and Omana (Mal. *ōmana*).

Then Captain Hamilton describes the visit of the prince on his ship:

> I carried him to the great Cabin, and would have treated him with Coffee, Tea and Wine or Spirits, but he would taste none, telling me, that my Water was polluted by our Touch, but he thanked me. (. . .) This Prince, and his Predecessors, have been Lords of the Seas, Time out of Mind, and all trading Vessels between Cape *Comerin* and *Damaan*, were obliged to carry his passes. (. . .) but

[205] There are two branches of the family now: Ayancheri (Mal. *āyañcēri*) and Edavalat Kovilakams (Mal. *eṭavalattŭ kōvilakam*) (Sreedhara Menon 2014: 172).

[206] Due to an editorial mistake this part of Hamilton's journey to Malabar was put in the second volume of his travel accounts, whereas it should be inserted in the first one.

> when the *Portugueze* settled in *India*, then they pretended to the Sovereignty of the Seas, which occasioned a War between him and and them, that has lasted ever since. (...) He stayed about three Hours on board, and, at his going away, I presented him with five Yards of scarlet Cloth, a small Carpet, a Fowling-piece and a Pair of Pistols finely gilt, which Present he seemed highly pleased with; and he took a *Manila*, or Wrist-jewel off from his left Arm, on which was engraven something of their Language, in their own characters, and putting it on my left Arm, declared me a free Denizon in all his Territories (...) he was a very well shaped Man, about 40 Years of Age, of a very dark Colour, but not quite black, his Eyes very lively and sparkling, and something of a majestick Air in his Deportment.
> (*Hamilton 1995 II: 299–301*)

Hamilton interestingly described also his second meeting with the prince, this time in the palace, which according to Captain Hamilton was meanly built but clean and neat. They were talking about the ruler's clearly expressed wish to cooperate with the English East India Company. Hamilton met the prince once more, in 1707, landing in the place which he called Mealie (Mayyali = Mahé).

After the arrival of the Portuguese in Kerala, naval encounters between them and Kadattanad became frequent but as Hamilton stated:

> (...) the *Portugueze* got Footing in all the Dominions of the Princes whose Lands reach to the Sea-shore, yet they never could get a Foot of Ground in the *Balanores* Country, tho' many Trials have been made, and fair Means used to effect it.
> (*Hamilton 1995 II: 305*)

But the French finally were welcomed there, too. In 1721, it was "(...) the Prince of Bargaret (French version of Badagara/Vaṭakara name—LS) that had started the ball rolling for the French at Mahé" and the treaty "with the Bayanor, Prince of Bargaret", was signed on 2 April 1721 (Ray 2004: 655). The French had the permission to establish their base in Mahé, i.e. Mealie of Hamilton's account, and another piece of land was promised to them.

Due to the instigations of the English, this permission soon was withdrawn. The English presented the ruler of Kadattanad as a rebel subject of the Kolattiris, who had no rights to cede the land. The French did not quit and all sorts of plots were introduced. We hear about secret sympathizers of France (certain *nambyārs* and a younger brother of the prince) and the spies at the court of Kadattanad, as well as the prince's spies in Pondicherry (Ray 2004: 666–667). Finally, only in 1725 did the French settle in Mahé for good, not even asking the prince for his opinion anymore. The Englishmen were not happy about such a development and soon clashes started. From the entries in the diary of the Tellicherry (Anglicized form < Mal. *talaśśēri/talaccēri*) factory referred to by Logan, we understand that the ruler of Kadattanad was clever enough to play off one factory against the other.

To protect their trade English factors resolved to assist Kadattanad with money, as being cheaper than war (Logan 1981 I: 406).

Finally, both factories achieved an agreement executed on 9th March and 17th and 28th April 1728. But it was not the end of serious conflicts because in 1740 the political situation in Europe created tension between French and English traders. Also Kadattanad was involved in fighting. On 5th and 18th September 1740, the French were defeated by them. However, in the next year, in November, fortune favoured the French. The English intervened and according to the agreement they were supposed to arbitrate in case of any conflict between the French and Kadattanad rulers (Logan 1981 I: 426). Still, there was no permanent peace in the region but soon another powerful player in the Malabar game appeared.

In February 1766, Hyder Ali of Mysore reached Mangalore and started his march to the coast of Malabar. The Raja of Chirakkal and his family sought shelter in Tellicherry. The victorious army met an organised opposition only in Kadattanad, however, the Raja's soldiers, unable to face the impetuous attack and tactics unknown to them, were defeated. The battle was depicted by one of the invaders and this work was later edited by Prince Ghulam Muhammad Khan, the last surviving son of Tipu Sultan. The Malabar, especially after the suicidal death of the Zamorin, was open to Mysore forces. The Kadattanad family was able to regain their realm at that time, paying a substantial sum to the invader, as other Rajas did. From 1774 the ruler of Kadattanad was a feudatory of Hyder Ali (Logan 1981: 502). Certain rulers, with the assistance of the English, rebelled against Mysorean authorities established by Hyder Ali but the Company stopped the hostility towards invaders, which made the local princes helpless. The Kolattiris, who were loyal to Hyder Ali, marched against Kadattanad and the senior Raja, who was an adherent of the English, was replaced by a young prince (Kareem 1973: 63). By November 1779 all British troops were concentrated in Tellicherry to defend the town against Kadattanad and Kolattunad Rajas. In 1780 it became obvious that Hyder Ali had planned a war against the English. In 1782 the English could celebrate a great victory over Mysore and at that point some local chiefs joined them. In June 1782 Hyder Ali's son, Tipu, marched to the Malabar Coast with his forces but the news about his father's death broke up his campaign; appointing a governor, he hastened back. In 1788, when Tipu Sultan again marched towards coastal countries, the king of Kadattanad with his family sought shelter in Tellicherry, and from there he had taken a boat to Travancore.[207] He entered into a pact with the English, agreeing to take a united stand against Tipu. In 1790 the king returned to his realm and Tipu left Malabar to never come back. But now the Company was dictating its conditions:

> (...) the three northern Rajas did not immediately acquiesce in the Company's sovereignty over them, but after some hesitation they soon found the necessity of relaxing their pretentions, and the

[207] The Kuttipuram fort was still defended. It was one of the last places in Malabar to hold out for Tipu, nevertheless in 1789 it was captured (Innes 1933: 463).

> Kadattanad Raja was the first to agree to a settlement on 25th April 1792 (...).
> (*Logan 1981: 537*)

1.2 Kadattanad Rajas as patrons and literati

The political situation in the region stabilized in the next decades. Perhaps this was the reason why the Kadattanad rulers increased their interest in promoting local culture. They were ardent supporters of *kathakaḷi* (Mal. < Skt. *kathā*—story + *kaḷi*—play, game) or dance-drama art and there was even an earlier distinctive dance style known as *kaṭattanāṭu* (Zarrilli 2000: 26, 246).

Later on, at the turn of the 19th and 20th centuries, the contribution of Kadattanad Rajas to the cultural legacy of the country, themselves poets and patrons of various artists, writers and eminent scholars, was even greater. Sankaravarman Raja, who was popularly known as Appu Tampuran (1774–1838), contributed to diverse subjects, such as astrology, astronomy, mathematics and architecture. His and Sridevi Kettilamma's (Mal. *keṭṭilamma*) son, Kunjunni Kurup (1813–1885), belonging to the Kunniyur (Mal. *kunniyūr*) family, was the author of several Sanskrit works, such as the *Devīmāhātmya* and a messenger poem the *Kapotasandeśa*.

Udayavarman (1864–1906), a writer himself, was a patron of a Sanskrit scholar and author of many works in Sanskrit, namely Nilakanthan Mussat (Mal. *nīlakaṇṭhan mūssat*) (1867–1946), as well as Krishna Variyar (1867–1936), who wrote a poem in four cantos describing the coronation of the king of Cochin, entitled *Śrīrāmavarmamāharājābhiṣeka* (Kunjunni Raja 1980: 264, 267–269). A great number of ancient and modern works were published due to his initiative. He even founded a printing press. Also the literary magazine *Kavanodayam* appeared under his patronage (Krishna Menon 1990: 83). In 1896 he established the

Raja's High School in Purameri (Fig. 39, p. 175).[208] In 1904 he took the initiative in conducting a literary gathering at Brennen College in Tellicherry. Among the great poets who participated in the literary discussions periodically organized by him were for instance Narayana Menon[209] of Vallathol, or Ullur. Ullur, encouraged by him, started translating Sanskrit classics into vernacular. Udayavarman translated or commented on some Sanskrit works but also wrote in Sanskrit and Malayalam. He authored a *bhaṇa*, a one-actor and one-act play, entitled *Rasikabhūṣaṇa* (Kunjunni Raja 1980: 269).

Another member of this family—Ravivarman (1871–1913)—wrote a century of verses known as *Anyāpadeśaśataka*. For once, this contribution to Sanskrit Kerala literature was published in 1910 in Tanjore (Anglicized form < Tam. *tañcāvūr*) as well as the collection of his short poems (Aeswaran Nampoothiry 1972: 105).

It should also be mentioned that in Kadattanad military training and physical excercises went in pair with intellectual development.

> A kalari is an institution common to all parts of Malabar, but the people of the northern part will tell you with pardonable pride that it prevails mostly in their midst and is most popular in the Kaḍaṭṭanād locality, the scene of several deeds of daring of a great hero named Ṭacchōli Oṭēnan, who is said to have once jumped across a well, 66 feet in circumference. This well, which stands near the town of Badagara, is still pointed out by the people as a relic of past greatness.
> (*Padmanabha Menon 1993: 475–476*)

---

[208] In the *Madras District Gazetteers. Malabar.* Vol. 1, one can read: "The Ayancheri and Edavalat *kovilagams* and the palace of Elaya Raja of Kadattanad family are in Purameri amsam, where the Elaya Raja maintains a high school" (Innes 1933: 463).

[209] *Mēnōn/Mēnavan/Mēnokki* (Mal.)—a caste title of a section of the Nayars or a title given by the king to a nobleman, or an accountant, superintendent, minister.

The hero mentioned above was praised in the "Northern Ballads"[210] and his legend is connected with the Lokanarkavu (Mal. *lōkanārkāvu˘*) temple, which belonged to the Kadattanad Royal Family (Fig. 40, p. 175). The Lokanarkavu Bhagavati patronises the performers of Kalarippayattu,[211] Kerala martial art.

2. Lakshmi Tampuratti prays for progeny

Lakshmi Tampuratti, born in 1845 at the Eṭavalattu˘ Kōvilakam (Fig. 41, p. 176) nearby Purameri, holds an important place among the royal literati. She was well-versed in Sanskrit and wrote many poems. Some of them were published by the *Vijñanacintāmaṇi* printing press established by Punnasseri Nambi[212] Neelakantha Sharma (Mal. *punnaśśēri nampi nīlakaṇṭha śarmā*) (1858–1934), an eminent writer and scholar and her close friend. It seems, however, that only one of her Sanskrit works has been preserved. It was published in 1931 by Italian scholar Mario Vallauri and translated into Italian. In 1940 J. B. Chaudhari included the Sanskrit text into his second volume of *The Contribution of Women to Sanskrit Literature*, then the poem has been forgotten.

The plot known from the *Bhāgavatapurāṇa* 10.86 has already been introduced while discussing the poem of Manku Tampuran under the same title.[213] However, the work of Lakshmi Tampuratti is much longer.

---

210 In the *Madras District Gazetteers. Malabar.* Vol. I, Taccholi Otenan is called "the Robin Hood of Northern Malabar" and it is stated that: "many ballads still sung by coolies at their work commemorate his exploits" (Innes 1933: 462).

211 (Mal. *kaḷarippayattu˘*); read more about it, as well as about Taccholi Otenan, in Zarrilli 2010.

212 Mal. *nampi*—an inferior Brahmin or Ambalavasi.

213 I give the examples from the *Santānagopālam* authored by Manku in this chapter only to show its simplicity in wording as well as in metrical patterns, although written in correct language and transmitting the sense of

Lakshmi Tampuratti's *Santānagopālakāvya* consists of three chapters called *sargas*. There are 43 stanzas in the first chapter, the second one contains 37 strophes and the last one 50 couplets, altogether it counts 130 stanzas. Sanskrit theoreticians of literature (for instance Daṇḍin in his *Kāvyādarśa* or Bhāmaha in the *Kāvyālaṅkāra*) prescribe that *mahākāvyas* (Sanskrit court epic poems) should be composed in chapters called *sargas*. However, judging by its length, the work could be classified as belonging to *laghukāvya*, if not for the presence of *sargas*[214] and perhaps some other traits. Let us compare the way of presenting the plot in the first chapter of the *Santānagopālakāvya* by Lakshmi Tampuratti and the *Bhāgavatapurāṇa*.

> prathamaḥ sargaḥ /
> *āsīc chriyā vijitanirjararājapuryāṃ*
> *kaścit purā dvijavaraḥ kila kṛṣṇapuryām /*
> *so 'yaṃ svadharmanirataḥ saha dharmapatnyā*
> *reme sukhaṃ haripadāmbujadattacittaḥ //1//*
>
> Once upon a time, in the capital of Kṛṣṇa,
> exceeding in splendor the city of Indra,
> lived certain Brahmin, who with his mind focused
> on the lotus feet of Viṣṇu and occupied
> with his own duties, enjoyed marital relations.
>
> *kālena kaścana suto 'pi ca tasya jātaḥ*
> *kālasya hanta vaśatāṃ sa tadaiva yātaḥ*
> *ādāya tanmṛitaśarīram upetya śauriṃ*
> *śokāturo bahutaraṃ vilalāpa vipraḥ //2//*

---

the Puranic story.

[214] According to Bhāmaha, theortician of Sanskrit literature:

> *Kāvyālaṅkāra* 1.19ab
> *sargabandho mahākāvyam mahatām ca mahac ca yat /*
> *A Mahākāvya* consists of chapters (called *sargas*);
> it is lengthy and for the great (i.e. it treats about the great personages).
> (*Naganatha Sastry (ed.) 1991: 7*)

In due time a son was born to him,
but, alas! he got into Yama's power.
Carrying his dead body, he went to Kṛṣṇa.
Brahmin, very distressed by regret, lamented:

hāhā hare! jagadadhīśa kṛpāmburaśe
pādāravindavinatāvanalolupātman /
pāpātmano mama suto 'yam abhud gatāsuḥ
śrīvāsudeva sadayaṃ paripālayainam //3//

"Ah! Hari! Lord of the World! Ocean of Mercy!
Ah, you, whose mind is eager to protect
those bowing to your lotus feet!
A son of mine, who am a sinner, lost his life!
Ah, son of Vasudeva, save him by mercy!

rāmādayo yaduvarāś ca madīyacitta-
tāpāpanodanakṛte kuruta prasādam /
loke 'tra duṣkaram aho bhavatāṃ na kiñcid
devaś ca saṃprati nideśakṛto yato vaḥ //4//

You, Balarāma and others,
the greatest of the descendants of Yadu!
Give the grace to remove the torments of my heart.
Nothing is difficult in this world for you,
for the gods are now obeying you."

ityādi tasya ruditaṃ niśamayya sarve
kṛṣṇādayo 'pi ca tadā yaduvaṃśamukhyāḥ /
tūṣṇiṃ sthitāḥ kila jane viparītadaive
nūnaṃ bhavanti bata sādhujanāś ca vāmāḥ //5//

All of them: Kṛṣṇa and the most important of
the Yadu race, having calmed his incessant cry, fell silent.
Indeed, when fate is against man, alas!, even good people
are just powerless.

dṛṣṭvā tu śiṣṭaparipālananaṣṭabhāvān
ruṣṭo jagāda punar apy avanīsurendraḥ /
kaṣṭaṃ prajā mama ca saṃprati śiṣṭamārga-
juṣṭasya dhṛṣṭanṛpadhauṣṭyavaśāt pranaṣṭāḥ //6//

Seeing those who gave up their intention
to protect the learned man, angry Brahmin said again:
"Alas! The offspring of mine, who am practising
the ordered path, died, because of
the wickedness of the insolent king.

kliśyanti yat sutadhanādivināśahetor
viprādayo 'pi ca paraṃ bhuvi vṛttavantaḥ /
tasyātra patyur avivekabhavaṃ dharitryā
daurātmyam eva hi nidānam udāharanti //7//

That the Brahmins and others, possessing virtues in
the highest degree on earth, suffer, because of
the loss of children, property, etc., as the main reason
pointed out, is the iniquity of the king originating
from inability to discriminate.

sādhāraṇo na jagatīti bhavatprabhāvaḥ
sarvair yad ucyata ihācyuta satyam etat /
yasmāt svapakṣajanadarśitapakṣapātaḥ
saṃdṛśyate taditareṣu na mādṛśeṣu //8//

Oh, Imperishable!
Your efficacy is not the same in the world. It is true
what everyone is saying here. This manifests in
relation to other people, not to such ones as me,
because of siding with people in your own party.

putraṃ purā yamapurāt svaguroḥ pranaṣṭaṃ
hṛtvāpi kṛṣṇa kalitā kila dakṣiṇāsya//
āhṛtya kaṃsanihatān api ṣat kumārān
mātuḥ pradarśya tarasāpahṛto viṣādaḥ //9//

In the past, oh Kṛṣṇa, as a reward for teaching,
you fetched the deceased son of your *guru* from the
city of Yama. Bringing the six sons killed by Kaṃsa
to their mother, you quickly removed her despair.

paitāmahāstranihataṃ gurunandanasya
pārthātmajātmajam athāpi ca garbhasaṃstham /
cakrāyudhena bhavatā parirakṣya samyag
vyaktīkṛtaiva nijamitrajaneṣu maitrī //10//

Having saved with your discus the grandson
of Arjuna, who was killed by Brāhma's weapon
belonging to the son of the royal preceptor, you truly
showed benevolence towards your friends.

kiṃ cātra ṣoḍaśasahasramitā mahiṣyaḥ
saṃprāptaputradaśakā bhavato hi sarvāḥ /
kiṃ vā vacobhir adhikair akhilaṃ tad etad
ātmaṃbharitvamahimādhikajṛmbhitaṃ te //11//

Moreover, all your wives, sixteen thousand in
number, had ten sons. What can one say more?
It all reveals the magnitude of your selfishness."

evaṃ vilapya suciraṃ yadupuṃgavānāṃ
bhāvaṃ nirīkṣya ca tadā vigatānukūlyam /
so 'yaṃ dvijo nijagṛhaṃ prati sannivṛttaḥ
śokaṃ niyamya dayitāsahito nyavātsīt //12//

Lamenting in this way for a long time and
noticing a lack of sympathy of the best of
the Yadavas, at that time this Brahmin returned
to his home and, having eased his sadness,
lived with his wife.

bhūyo 'pi bhūsuravaraḥ kramaśo vinaṣṭān
aṣṭau tathaiva tanayān api kṛṣṇapārśvam /
nītvā pureva sa śucā vilapan punaś ca
prasthāya duḥsthahṛdayaḥ svagṛhe 'vatasthe //13//

And anew, in this way the noble Brahmana
brought to Kṛṣṇa eight dead sons,
one after another. As before, he was wailing in despair,
then again leaving and staying at home with heartache.

atrāntare svajanakarmaṇi yādavānāṃ
prītyai sametya nivasann amarendraputraḥ /
śrutvā sute 'sya navame 'pi mṛte vilāpaṃ
viprasya niḥsahamanā vacanaṃ babhāṣe //14//

At that time Arjuna, out of the affection for his relatives,
Yādavas, arrived at their sacrificial ceremony.

Hearing the Brahmin's complaint when his ninth son died,
unable to resist, he said:

bhūpaḥ kim atra na hi bhūsurarakṣaṇāya
yāgaprasaktahṛdayā yadavo dvijāḥ kim /
te 'pi śvasanti bata bhastryupamaṃ mahīśā
ye santyajanty asuguṇān na mahīsurārthaṃ //15//

"Why is there no king here to protect the splendid Brahmins?
Why do twice-born descendants of Yadu have their minds focused
on religious sacrifices? Unfortunately, those lords of the earth
who do not abandon essential principles for the good of the gods
on the earth (i.e. Brahmins), pant like bellows.

śokaṃ tyaja dvijavaraivam itaḥ paraṃ te
jāto bhaved yadi sutaḥ sahasāham enam /
neṣyāmi taṃ yamam api prasabhaṃ vijitya
jahyāṃ na cet sadhanur eva tanuṃ hutaśe //16//

Give up sadness, oh splendid Brahmin! If, starting from today,
you have a child and I do not take him immediately after defeating
Yama with all force, I will throw my body and bow into the fire!"

itthaṃ tu tasya vacanaṃ niśamayya jiṣṇor
ṇātyantatuṣṭahṛdayas tam uvāca vipraḥ /
kiṃ vā dhanaṃjaya vijalpasi sāṃprataṃ hā
nirlajjam eva yadurājasabhāntarāle //17//

Hearing these words of the victorious Arjuna, the Brahmin,
with an unhappy heart, said to him:
"Why, O Arjuna, now, in the middle of the gathering
of the Yādava ruler, do you speak so shamelessly?

kṛṣṇādibhiś ca bhuvanaprathitaprabhāvair
atyantaduṣkaratame 'tra kathaṃ prabhus tvam /
dantīndramastakavidāraṇacaṇḍaśauryān
kaṇṭhīravān samatigacchati kiṃ śṛgālaḥ //18//

In this extremely difficult matter,
how can you be equal to Kṛṣṇa
and others famous in the world for their power?
The jackal does not approach the lions that dare
to tear apart the temples of mighty elephants.

janmāntarārjitaśubhāśubhakarmahetoḥ
saṃjātam atra bhuvi janmavatāṃ sukhādi
kaḥ pauruṣair iha vilaṃghayituṃ kṣamaḥ syāt
ko vādya pārtha tava bālyamadātirekaḥ //19//

Because of good or bad karma gained in previous lives,
happiness, etc. of the living beings manifests itself in this world.
Who on this earth, through human actions,
would be able to overcome this?
Or, who would now have your childish haughtiness, oh Arjuna?"

ity ūcuṣo 'sya viśayaṃ parihartum eva
niḥśeṣato nijabalaṃ praśaśaṃsa pārthaḥ /
mā mā kṛthā mayi vṛthā pṛthivīsuraivaṃ
śaṅkāṃ samastajanatāvinutānubhāve //20//

To dispel the doubts of the speaker completely,
Arjuna extolled his own power:
"Do not, oh Brahmin, do not rise false doubts
about me, whose dignity is spread by entire community/population.

kṛṣṇo 'ham asmi na ca tatsahajo na rāmaḥ
kārṣṇyādayo 'pi ca tathā yadūvaṃśamukhyāḥ /
jānīhi māṃ suravarātmajam ātmabāhu-
vīryaprasāditagirīśagṛhītaśastram //21//

I am not Kṛṣṇa, nor his brother Balarāma,
nor a descendant of Kṛṣṇa or others,
nor any of the leaders of the Yadu clan.
Recognize in me the son of Indra,
the one who received weapons from Śiva,
pleased with the power of my arms.

bhittvā purā nṛpavarair akhilair abhedyaṃ
lakṣyaṃ mayā hy apahṛtā drupadendraputrī /
gatvottarāṃ diśam aśeṣamahīśvarāṇāṃ
kṛtvā padaṃ ca mukuṭeṣu karo gṛhītaḥ //22//

Once I hit the target unattainable for
all splendid rulers and took Drupada's daughter.
I went to the north, put my foot on the tiaras
of all kings and married (her).

sīrāyudhādibhir atāryatamo nitāntaṃ
yādobhir eṣa bhayado 'pi ca dānavā[215]*bdhiḥ /*
tīrṇaḥ kṣaṇena hṛdayākalitorubhadrā-
vakṣojakumbhayugalena mayā kṣameṇa //23//

The terrifying ocean with sea monsters and Dānavas,
completely impossible to cross for Balarāma and others,
I crossed immediately, with a pair of pots[216]
like the breasts of Subhadra tied to the chest.

tātājñayā divam upetya nihatya daityān
kaumāraśaktisukhaviśramadānaśauṇḍam /
adyāpi siddhataruṇīnivahaiḥ samodaṃ
saṃstūyate caritam adbhutam asmadīyam //24//

After defeating Daityas, at the Father's command,
I entered the heavens, and even today,
a host of Siddha maidens praise my amazing deeds,
which ensured a pleasant rest for Kumāra's energy.

vācā kim adya mama bhāratasaṃgare prāg
gāṅgeyamukhyarathikān akhilān vijitya /
dhātrī samudraraśanāpahṛtā tad etan
nāśrāvi hanta bhuvi viśrutam atra sarvam //25//

What should I say now?
After defeating all in the Bharatas' war:
the best warriors on chariots and Bhishma,
the land surrounded by the ocean was taken away.
Alas, all this is not celebrated here, on earth ?!

āśvasyatāṃ svagṛham etya madīyavāgbhir
āśvāsyatāṃ ca dayitā pṛthivīsurendra /
āsannasūtisamayāṃ tu nivedayaināṃ
āpannasūnuharaṇe vidito 'stu pārthaḥ //26//

---

[215] Em.: *yādava.*

[216] Such a way of crossing the rivers is attested in Indian literature (e.g. tragic love story from Punjab about Sohni Mahiwal, who swims every night across the river using an earthenware vessel in order to meet her beloved). On the other hand, the comparison of woman's breasts to pots belongs to a conventional set of metaphors used in *kāvya* tradition.

After coming home, may my words give you comfort
and let your wife take courage, oh Brahmin!
Inform me when she is close to childbirth.
Let Arjuna be present if the abduction
of a newborn child is to occur."

niḥśaṃkam eva gaditāṃ giram arjunasya
viśvasya cetasi bhṛśaṃ sa tu vipravaryaḥ /
sadyaḥ sametya sadanaṃ gṛhiṇīm ca samyag
āśvāsayan katipayāni dināny anaiṣīt //27//

Trusting firmly in his heart in Arjuna's words
spoken with confidence, indeed, this splendid Brahmin
immediately went home, comforted his wife entirely
and spent a few days with her.

kāle tu tatra dayitāṃ paripūrṇasattvām
ālokya bhūsuravareṇa gṛhaṃ pranītaḥ /
ācchādya tannilayanaṃ viśikhair mahāstraiḥ
pārthaḥ prasūtisamayaṃ pratipālya tasthau //28//

At the appropriate time, seeing his wife
in advanced pregnancy, the illustrious Brahmin
brought Arjuna home. He, covering her shelter
with arrows and powerful missiles,
awaited the time of labour.

jate tadā yuvatilokavilāpaghoṣaiḥ
sākaṃ vibhidya śarakūṭam amuktadehe /
yāte divaṃ nijasute dvijasattamena
śokātureṇa jagade vijayaḥ saroṣam //29//

When after the birth, which was accompanied
by the screams and laments of women and the firing
of a mass of arrows, his own son ascended
into the sky with his body, the respectable Brahmin
overwhelmed with regret, spoke to Arjuna with anger:

he phālgunārjuna pṛthāsutakṛṣṇabandho
kutrāsi śakrasuta vikramavāriraśe /
ādyaiva sādhu vidito bhujavikramas te
sadyo gataḥ satanur eva yataḥ śiśur me //30//

"Oh Phālguna! Oh Arjuna, son of Pṛthā,
oh relative of Kṛṣṇa!
Where are you? Son of Indra, ocean of bravery!
Today the power of your arms has been well demonstrated,
because my son in an instant left with his body!

sa tvaṃ yamātmajamarutsutayoḥ sagarbhyas
tyaktaḥ kathaṃ bhavasi satyaparākramābhyām /
hantorvaśīprathitaśāpabaloditaṃ tat
ṣaṇḍhatvam eva bhajasīty adhunāpi manye //31//

Why has truth and courage left you—a brother
of the son of the God of Wind and the son
of the God of Death? Woe! You are affected
by the impotence caused by
the power of curse pronounced by Urvaśī,
I think now.

gaṇḍīva eṣa tava khāṇḍavadāhalabdho
nānāripupravaraśauryavimāthivīryaḥ /
saṃsargatas tava kim asya ca ṣaṇḍhateti
matvā napuṃsakatayāpi ca kathyate 'sau //32//

Your bow Gaṇḍīva obtained for burning
the forest of Khāṇḍava,
having the power to destroy the excellent
heroism of different adversaries—is its
asexuality due to the relationship with you?
Reasoning so, Gaṇḍīva's gender
was defined as neuter.[217]

dehas tavāyam adhunā dahane hutaś cet
khedaṃ mukundasahajaiva bhajen nitāntam /
kṛṣṇā punaś ca patibhiś caturaiś caturbhir
niṣṇātadhīr atitarāṃ sukhitaiva sā syāt //33//

---

[217] Stanza refers to an episode of *Mahābhārata*, when Arjuna was hiding at the court of King Virāṭa, acting as his daughter's dance teacher-eunuch. The *gāṇḍīva* noun denoting a bow (as well as a particular bow, belonging to Arjuna), can occur in two grammatical genders: masculine and neuter.

If your body were now offered to the fire,
Subhadra, Kṛṣṇa's sister, would suffer
a lot, but Draupadī, with thoughts absorbed
with four fit men, would be very happy."

ityādiduḥsahavacoviśikhaughaviddho
duḥkhākulaḥ sa khalu śakrasutas tadānīm /
vidyābalena nilayād avanīsurasya
mānī yayau yamapurīṃ harim apy adṛṣṭvā //34//

Then overwhelmed with sadness, pierced by words
difficult to bear like by flood of arrows,
this son of Indra, having his dignity wounded,
by magic power, without even seeing Kṛṣṇa,
moved from the house of Brahmin to the city of Yama.

sammānapūrvam amunā pratidarśiteṣu
sammargayaṃs tata ito nirayeṣu pārthaḥ /
tadvat krameṇa nilayeṣv api dikpatīnāṃ
kutrāpy adṛṣṭaśiśur eṣa yayau viṣādam //35//

Yama showed him around with respect; he searched in hell,
also in turn at the headquarters of the guardians
of the directions of the world. He was worried,
seeing the baby nowhere.

bhūyo vicintya bahuśaḥ svayaśovināśaṃ
bhūritrapāparavaśaḥ sa bhṛśaṃ manasvī /
draṣṭuṃ śaśāka na yato nijabāndhavādyāṃs
tyaktuṃ tataḥ svatanum aicchad ayaṃ kṛśānau //36//

He thought a lot and constantly about losing his own fame.
He, overwhelmed by great shame, could not turn to Kṛṣṇa
and other relatives and in consequence he wanted
to throw his body into the fire.

sandīpya tatra dahanaṃ bhṛśam indhanaughaiḥ
sañcintya cāpi puravairipadābjam antaḥ /
yāvaj juhāva dahane svatanuṃ sa jiṣṇus
tāvat sametya harinābhidadhe nirudhya //37//

He lit a great fire from heaps of glades,
meditating in the meantime on the lotus feet

of Viṣṇu. When Arjuna was offering his body
to the fire, then Kṛṣṇa came,
stopped him and said:

mā mā kuruṣva kurusattama sāhasaṃ ma-
yy asmin bhavatpriyasakhe 'pi ca jīvatīttham /
hā hanta bhūritarakīrtinidānabhūtaṃ
dehaṃ vihātum iha kas tava durvicāraḥ //38//

"No, don't do that inconsiderately,
oh, the best from the race of Kuru,
when I, your dear friend, live here!
Ah, such carelessness on your part to give up
your own body, which is the actual cause of your immense fame.

kṛtsnaṃ mahītalam aho tava hastasaṃsthaṃ
svarlokadurlabha ihādya tu bhogayogaḥ /
kṛṣṇo 'smy ahaṃ ca bhavataḥ hitaiṣī
na jñāyate vijaya saṃprati śokahetuḥ //39//

All the earth is in your hands!
And access to such pleasures as here
and now is difficult in heaven. I, Kṛṣṇa,
desire prosperity for you, oh Arjuna!
The cause of your sadness is just unknown to me.

kṛcchre purāpi ca pṛthā-suta tatra tatra
yad yan mayā hy upakṛtaṃ bhavato hitārthe
vismṛtya tat sakalam apy ayi māṃ anuktvā
tyaktuṃ kalevaram aho bata kiṃ tavāsīt //40//

Woe! how could it happen to you, oh son of Pṛthā,
to give up your body without telling me anything after all that
I did in difficult cases in the past for your sake?"

vācaṃ niśamya madhurāṃ madhusūdanasya
devaṃ nyavedayad amuṃ vijayaḥ saśokam /
jānann apīttham akhilaṃ khalu sarvavedin
naivaṃ pralobhayitum arhasi dāsam enam //41//

Arjuna, who heard Kṛṣṇa's affectionate speech,
said to the king sadly: "Knowing the whole matter,

Oh All-knowing One! surely you should not tempt
me—(your) servant this way.

rakṣiṣyate dvijatanūja itīriteyaṃ
vyarthābhavat sapadi hanta mama pratijñā /
tyakṣyāmi tat tanum imāṃ hatakīrtir agnau
tasmāt prasīda jagadīśvara dehy anujñām //42//

Ah, the promise that the son of the Brahmin would be saved,
once uttered, immediately became vain.
So I, whose fame has been ruined,
will throw this body into fire.
Therefore, have mercy, Lord of the World! give your consent!"

tyaja vijaya viṣādaṃ sāṃpratam sarvam eva
priyasakha tarasā te vāñchitaṃ sādhayiṣye" /
iti sumadhuravācā sāntvayitvā tam enaṃ
karatalam avalambya prasthito vāsudevaḥ //43//

"Ah, Arjuna! give up all your worries now. Dear friend!
I will grant your wishes quickly."
So after comforting him with gentle words
and taking his hand, the son of Vasudeva went away.

iti prathamaḥ sargaḥ /[218]

Here is the first chapter.

When we compare the story told by Lakshmi Tampuratti with that contained in the *Bhāgavatapurāṇa*, because it is undoubtedly its source, it turns out that they essentially convey the same content. However, in the first chapter of the *Santānagopālakāvya*, as many as 43 stanzas lead us to the same moment which is presented in the *Bhāgavatapurāṇa*'s 23-stanza-long narrative. The whole story of the poor Brahmin is encompassed in the *Bhāgavata* in 41 stanzas, which is even less than the *Santānagopālakāvya*'s first chapter and

[218] The text of two other *sargas* is provided in the Appendix on the basis of its two previous editions: by Vallauri (1931) and Chaudhari (1940).

also the third one. What, then, makes the story as depicted by Lakshmi longer?

The *Bhāgavatapurāṇa* narrative briefly communicates the subsequent events, building up in short dialogues and monologues of the characters. Lakshmi is expanding the dialogic parts. Suffice to mention the following two examples.

The Brahmin lamenting and accusing Kṛṣṇa for being the direct cause of the death of his progeny in the *Bhāgavata* says only two sentences:

BhP 10.86
brahmadviṣaḥ śaṭhadhiyo lubdhasya viṣayātmanaḥ /
kṣatrabandhoḥ karmadoṣāt pañcatvaṃ me gato 'rbhakaḥ //23//
hiṃsāvihāraṃ nṛpatiṃ duḥśīlam ajitendriyam /
prajā bhajantyaḥ sīdanti daridrā nityaduḥkhitāḥ //24//[219]

"My boy died because of the evil deeds of this enemy
of Brahmins—the wicked-minded, covetous,
sensual Kshatriya. The subjects of a king
of evil character, who likes violence and is unable
to control his senses, are suffering,
poor and eternally unhappy."

Lakshmi composes a much longer speech by the Brahmin (from stanza 6 to stanza 11), who not only states that the subjects pay for the sins of their rulers, but in subsequent stanzas shows that Kṛṣṇa's attitude towards his relatives was completely different. Did he not bring back to life his *guru*'s son and the six sons of Devakī? Did he not save Arjuna's unborn grandson? Kṛṣṇa seems to be indifferent to the Brahmin's fate, because he is not one of his kin. The accusations addressed to Arjuna sound even harsher (SGK 1.30–33). Lakshmi brings the despair and anger of a father who loses children one by one closer to recipients of her poem. The audience can really sympathize with the drama of a childless Brahmin yearning for offspring.

[219] The text according to Shastree's edition (Shastree 1997).

Let us now compare the statements of Arjuna trying to show to the Brahmin his own extraordinary character, and especially bravery. In the *Bhāgavata* these are merely two stanzas:

> BhP. 10.86
> *nāhaṃ saṅkarṣaṇo brahman na kṛṣṇaḥ kārṣṇir eva ca /*
> *ahaṃ vā arjuno nāma gāṇḍīvaṃ yasya vai dhanuḥ //32//*
> *māvamaṃsthā mama brahman vīryaṃ tryambakatoṣaṇam /*
> *mṛtyuṃ vijitya pradhane āneṣye te prajāṃ prabho //33//*
>
> "Brahmin! I am not Samkarṣana,
> I am not Kṛṣṇa or a descendant of his.
> Indeed, I am Arjuna, whose bow is Gāṇḍiva.
> Do not belittle my bravery, oh Brahmin,
> the one who pleased the three-eyed god, Śiva.
> I will defeat death and bring you your offspring."

The same message, although expressed in a different set of words, was provided by the poetess; however, she expanded the speech of a proud warrior—Arjuna. In a passage of six and a half stanzas (SGK 1.20cd–26), Arjuna mentioned the most important evidences of his bravery, as for instance the defeat of the best warriors on the Kurukṣetra battlefield.

The speeches of the heroes, i.e. discursive fragments, are an extremely important element of the structure of each and every *mahākāvya*. They are intertwined with descriptions of either nature or the actions of the characters. Louis Renou has already drawn attention to this tendency, devoting his extensive and inspiring article "Sur La Structure Du Kāvya"to it (Renou 1959). Indira Viswanathan Peterson also underlines the presence of speeches of the heroes as well as descriptive passages in the *Kirātārjunīya* of Bhāravi.[220] In this way, Lakshmi provided her work with a salient feature of a *mahākāvya*, namely discursive passages and, besides, she equipped her poem with an indispensable,

[220] She devotes two important chapters to discuss the implementation and character of speeches in the *Kirātārjunīya*. These are chapters 4 and 5 (Viswanathan Peterson 2003: 47–66 and 67–88).

in the case of every *kāvya* work, property of creating aesthetic emotions.

As far as descriptive passages are concerned, the question arises of what they look like and whether they are present in the work of Lakshmi at all. The first canto was virtually deprived of them, although, for example, the mention of the capital of Kṛṣṇa "exceeding in splendor the city of Indra" (SGK 1.1) gave the opportunity to weave a longer conventional description of the city. Chaudhari in his short introduction preceding the edition of the *Santānagopālakāvya* text states:

> In this work we get some beautiful descriptions, e.g., of the Lokāloka mountain, Viṣṇu lying on the serpent Śeṣa, etc.
> (*Chaudhari 2001: 30*).

The descriptions mentioned by him are contained in the second chapter. Kṛṣṇa takes Arjuna to his chariot and they begin an extraordinary journey:

tato vyatīte 'drivare tu lokā-
lokābhidhe tatra tamo 'tighoram /
nivārya cakraprabhayā mahatyā
niruddhanetraṃ nijagāda pārtham //2//[221]

When they left the space around the mountain
called Lokāloka, [Kṛṣṇa] removing
the terrifying darkness by the glow of his discus,
said to the squinting Arjuna:

vilokyatām āśu vilokanīyaṃ
vilocanāsecanakaṃ janānām /
avarṇyatattanmahimātiśāyi
suparṇaketoḥ padam atyudāram //3//

"Look immediately at the truly sublime footprint of Him,
who has Garuḍa as a sign (Viṣṇu), beautiful,
delightful to the eyes of people,
abounding in indescribable greatness."

[221] The text of the whole second *sarga* in the Appendix.

Then the description continues until they were able to see (... *tau pradṛṣṭavantau...*—SGK 2.8b) and admire the divine figure visible before them:

phaṇīndraparyaṅkatale śayānaṃ
mahendranīlotpalamecakāṅgam /
kirīṭahārādivibhūṣaṇaugha
prakṛṣṭanānāmaṇidīpitāśam //9//

[They saw him] lying on the surface of a bed made
of a large snake (i.e. Śeṣa), with his body blue
from large sapphires reminding dark water lilies;
illuminating the space with various wonderful
jewels from the mass of his ornaments such
as necklace, tiara and others.

lalāṭadeśākalitordhvapuṇḍraṃ
kṛpārasāpūrṇasarojanetram /
suvarṇamīnopamakuṇḍalodyat-
prabhānuliptāmalagaṇḍaśobham //10//

[They saw him] with the sectarian mark on the forehead,
with the eyes full of the compassion sentiment just like
lotuses are full of nectar, with cheeks bright from
the glittering glow emanating from gold earrings reminding fish.

mṛdusmitoddyotimukhendubimbaṃ
galollasatkaustubhaśobhamānam /
caturbhujāsaktagadāriśaṅkha-
saroruhaṃ mañjulavanyamālam //11//

[They saw him] with the moon-like face illuminated
by a delicate smile, adorned by a jewel of *kaustubha*
throwing light on his neck, with four arms equipped
with a lotus, conch, discus and club,
with a charming forest garland.

svabhaktavātsalyaviśeṣaśaṃsi-
śrīvatsalakṣmāṅkitavatsadeśam /
anekapaṅkeruhasaṃbhavāṇḍa-
niveśaveśmāyitakukṣideśam //12//

[They saw him] with his chest marked with
the *śrīvatsa* sign, revealing
a particular sensitivity for his worshipers,
with abdomen part of his body arranged time
and again as the seat of Brahma contained in lotus.

pītāmbarācchāditapīvaroruṃ
pāpāndhakārāruṇapādapadmam /
nakhenduvidhvastasamastabhakta-
janāntarasthāyimahāndhakāram //13//

[They saw him] with his mighty thighs covered
with a yellow robe, feet like reddish lotuses
against the darkness of sin, with his toe nails
like the moon that dispel the thick darkness
that lies amongst all the followers.

sanatkumārādimunīndramukhyaiḥ
sanandamukhyair api pāriṣadyaiḥ /
surāsurādyair api mūrtimadbhir
nijāyudhaiḥ santatam īḍyamānam //14//

[They saw him] being constantly worshipped
by Sanatkumāra and other chiefs of great sages,
councilors headed by Sananda, as well as by gods
and demons etc. as well as by his own
personified weapons.

tadīyarūpāpahṛtākṣipadmāv
amū parānandapayodhimagnau
skhaladgirā tuṣṭuvatus tadānīṃ
jagadguruṃ pāṇḍavavāsudevau //15//

Then both, Arjuna and Kṛṣṇa, with lotus eyes
captivated by his beauty and immersed in the ocean
of great joy, praised him in a trembling voice.

Let us compare this excerpt again with the *Bhāgavatapurāṇa*. We find that the poetess does not mention that four horses of Kṛṣṇa, Śaibya, Sugrīva, Meghapuṣpa and Balāhaka, lost their way in the darkness and that is why it was necessary to provide some light using the discus, i.e. *cakra*.[222] The dramatic account of this part of the quest is reduced to one sentence only (SGK 2.2.). However, Lakshmi expands Puranic three-stanza fragment describing Viṣṇu to seven verses quoted above.

The *Bhāgavatapurāṇa* reads:

dadarśa tadbhogasukhāsanaṃ vibhuṃ
mahānubhāvaṃ puruṣottamottamam
sāndrāmbudābhaṃ supiśaṅgavāsasaṃ
prasannavaktraṃ rucirāyatekṣaṇam //54//

He saw the Lord of great might, seated comfortably
on him (i.e. on Śeṣa), the best among excellent
puruṣas, similar to a dense cloud,
in a beautiful yellow robe, with a kind face,
wide and beautiful eyes.

mahāmaṇivrātakirīṭakuṇḍala
prabhāparikṣiptasahasrakuntalam
pralambacārvaṣṭabhujaṃ sakaustubhaṃ
śrīvatsalakṣmaṃ vanamālayāvṛtam //55//

[He saw him] with a thousand scattered curls
bathed in the glow of mass of precious gems
from his crown and earrings, with eight beautiful
long arms, with *kaustubha* and the *śrīvatsa*
sign and covered with a forest garland.

sunandanandapramukhaiḥ svapārṣadaiś
cakrādibhir mūrtidharair nijāyudhaiḥ

---

[222] BhP 10.86

sapta dvīpān sasindhūṃś ca sapta sapta girīn atha
lokālokaṃ tathātītya viveśa sumahat tamaḥ //47//
tatrāśvāḥ śaibyasugrīvameghapuṣpabalāhakāḥ
tamasi bhraṣṭagatayo babhūvur bharatarṣabha //48//
tān dṛṣṭvā bhagavān kṛṣṇo mahāyogeśvareśvaraḥ
sahasrādityasaṅkāśaṃ svacakraṃ prāhiṇot puraḥ //49//
tamaḥ sughoraṃ gahanaṃ kṛtaṃ mahadvidārayad bhūritareṇa rociṣā //
manojavaṃ nirviviśe sudarśanaṃguṇacyuto rāmaśaro yathā camūḥ //50//
dvāreṇa cakrānupathena tat tamaḥ paraṃ paraṃ jyotir anantapāram
samaśnuvānaṃ prasamīkṣya phālgunaḥ pratāḍitākṣo pidadhe 'kṣiṇī ubhe //51//

puṣṭyāśriyā kīrtyajayākhilārdbhibhir
niṣevyamāṇam parameṣṭhināṃ patim //56//

[He saw him as] the Master of the lords of the world,
worshiped by his associates, with Nanda and Sunanda
at the head, by their own embodied weapons,
starting with cakra, by [his energies:] *puṣṭi*
or prosperity, *śrī* or auspiciousness, *kīrti*
or fame and by material world, as well as by all supernatural powers.

Both texts, the *Bhāgavatapurāṇa* and *Santānagopālakāvya* use the same technique in order to present the depiction of the god. Contrary to the common practice of closing the sense with each verse, the government of a verb over nouns is carried throughout several consecutive stanzas. In case of the *Bhāgavatapurāṇa* it is a fusion of three stanzas described in Sanskrit theory of literature as *sandānitaka* ("the chain"). In the *Santānagopālakāvya* it is a collection of seven stanzas, i.e. the so-called *kulaka* ("the multitude") containing from five to fifteen stanzas.[223]

The first and the last stanzas of the *sandānitaka* and *kulaka* respectively, contain the same message. Some words are repeated in both BhP 10.56 and SGK 2.15.

On the contrary, BhP 10.54 and SGK 2.9 differ considerably in the level of poetical sophistication, although they both show Viṣṇu lying on Śeṣa. The image created by Lakshmi shines and glitters even with an excess of gems, allowing the reader's imagination, though shaped on the basis of earthly experience, to create other worlds. In the compound word *mahendra-nīlotpala-mecakāṅgam*, as pointed out by J. B. Chaudhari, *nīla* is significantly put in the middle of it.

> It goes with the preceding and following parts; thus the meaning of the first part is mahendra-nīla-mecakāṅgam; and of the second, nīlotpala-mecakāṅgam /
> (*Chaudhary 2001, vol. 2: 62, ft.1*)

---

[223] More about such metrical short poems in Lienhard 1984: 66–67.

Such treatment saturates the image with shades of blue. Then Lakshmi adds bright colours to her palette, namely gold and white: gold earrings, lotus, face shining like the moon, smile on the face[224] (SGK 2.10 and 11).

While referring to Viṣṇu's lotus eyes full of compassion, in the compound *kṛpārasāpūrṇasarojanetram*, she plays on the double meaning of the word *rasa*: 1. an aesthetic emotion, 2. juice, nectar.

Verse 13 contrasts bright and dark colours. Darkness of sin, against which one can clearly see the yellow robe of Viṣṇu, his feet like vermillion lotuses and toe nails glistening like the moon. The message of the stanza is obvious: Viṣṇu is a patch of light in the thick darkness for which the followers should head.

The picture provided by Lakshmi is by no means static. We can admire the movements of light from gems and nails and the gold earrings in the shape of fish dangling on Viṣṇu's cheeks. Particularly the mention of earrings like fish lends the image grace and lightness. We see their movement against the background of dark skin and dark gems adorning the divine figure.

It should also be mentioned that the poetess in four consecutive stanzas (SGK 2.10–13) develops a description of God from head to toe nails. In stanza 10 his forehead, eyes and cheeks are described shortly. The next strophe shows his neck and arms. Then, in verse 12 his chest and abdomen are mentioned and finally, in stanza 13, his mighty thighs and feet with shining toe nails are visualized.

An essential feature of the epic poem (*mahākāvya*), and more broadly Sanskrit poetry (*kāvya*), is to describe the physical charms of the bodies of heroes, and more often heroines. A specific scheme for such descriptions is used by the poets, the so-called *nakhaśikha-varṇana* or *pādādikeśānta*. The poet begins the description with

[224] Smile, laughter (Skr. *hāsa*) and the aesthetic emotion *hāsya rasa* or comic sentiment have been connected with the colour white from the time of the *Nāṭyaśāstra* at least (about colours in the *Nāṭyaśāstra* see Kintaert 2005: 245–273).

toe nails of the young beauty and ends at the crown of her head. For the gods, however, the order should be opposite than in the case of human beings, that is from tip to toe. And that is the procedure which Lakshmi applies.

Again, for the sake of comparison, let us delve into the description offered by Manku Tampuran. Her *Santānagopālam* poem, as was mentioned above, is in a concise form of only 30 verses, that is less than the *Bhāgavatapurāṇa* offers, but two of them are devoted to outline Śeṣa (v. 25) and Viṣṇu's image as this is the core of the whole story—to visualize, address the god and ask Him for progeny. Viṣṇu on Śeṣa is adorated by Sunanda, Nanda and others[225] and he reminds a dark cloud:

tadbhogasaṃsthaṃ puruṣottamaṃ ca
kirīṭahārādivibhūṣitāṅgam /
pītāmbaraṃ padmaviśālanetraṃ
kālāmbudābhaṃ kamanīyarūpam //26//

[He saw] the most wonderful *puruṣa* on that snake,
in a beautiful form, with his body reminding a dark cloud
adorned with the diadem, necklace, etc., in yellow garment,
with large lotus eyes.

After presenting this picture Manku closes her recapitulation of the story, mentioning that the sons of the Brahmin returned to their parents and the idol was deposited in the Trippunitura temple.

When we compare the dialogic and descriptive parts of Lakshmi's poem, one more characteristic feature is revealed, typical of the techniques of writing both. In the dialogic passages of the work there are no long compounds, while descriptive ones abound in them. Only two compounds can create one stanza as in verse SGK 2.12. Still the language is elegant and easy to follow.

---

[225] Manku's *Santānagopālam*:

sunandanandādimahānubhāvaiś cakrādibhir mūrtidharaiḥ parītam /
dadarśa kṛṣṇas saha jiṣṇunā ca nanāma bhaktyā tam ananyarūpam //27//

Lakshmi Tampuratti employs various metres, especially at the end of each *sarga*, as was recommended for the poets composing *mahākāvyas*. J. B. Chaudhari provides information about different metres in the footnotes to the text edited by him.

The third canto abounds in rhyming or euphonic effects as *yamakas*[226] are used there.

In almost all the stanzas of this *sarga* the poetess uses the same pattern—in its last quarter the sequence of the same syllables repeats, of course phonemically identical parts have different morphemic analysis.

iha tu dīnaparāyaṇa sarvadā
yadupatiḥ sa dadātu hitaṃ tava /
nijavayovilaye 'pi ca yogināṃ
*a**sulabhaṃ sulabhaṃ** padam astu tat //9//*

iti vitirya tadāśiṣam agrato
madhuripuṃ ca samīkṣva mahīsuraḥ /
sudṛḍhabhaktiyutaḥ praṇipatya taṃ
*pa**ramudāram udāram** athāstuvat //10//*

Sometimes the pattern of repetition is more complicated:

*sa**madhikādhikam**oda**vidhā**yinaḥ*
*prati**vidhā**nam aho na jagattraye /*
***kim adhikaṃ** batadātum idaṃ jaga-*
*dv**ijaya te jayate** bhujavikramaiḥ //8//*

Taking all this into consideration, one can conclude that even if the work is short, it belongs to the genre of *sargabandha mahākāvya*.

Analyzing the content of the *Santānagopālakāvya*, it can be seen that the authoress demonstrates knowledge worthy of *paurāṇika*.[227] She not only reports the events described in the tenth book

---

[226] About *yamaka* read also the entries in Gerow's *Glossary of Indian Figures of Speech* (Gerow 1971: 223–238).

[227] About the lost world of *paurāṇikas* and *purāṇas* see Velcheru Narayana Rao 2005: 97–115.

of the *Bhāgavatapurāṇa*, but also retells a great number of information provided in other parts of it or in other *purāṇas*.

Nevertheless, still more interesting for our discourse is another stanza. In different genres pieces of personal information happen in different parts of the works. As far as the *sargabandha mahākāvya* is concerned, the usual practice, such as we find for example in Bhaṭṭi's *Rāvaṇavadha* (circa 7th c. CE), is to write just a sentence or two about the author and the circumstances of composing the poem at the end. In the case of the *ākhyāyikā* genre—that is a prose *mahākāvya*—the first chapters (*ucchvāsa*) are the place where some autobiographical narrative can be found. For instance, in the famous *Harṣacarita* by Bāṇa (7th c. CE) an account of the authors own early life and mentions of his ancestors are given in the first two *ucchvāsas*. Then events of King Harṣa's life follow. There is no such distinct genre as autobiography in Sanskrit *kāvya* tradition.

In Lakshmi Tampuratti's *Santānagopālakāvya* glimpses of the poetess's own life can be encountered in the last stanza of her poem:

rogārtayā 'pi ravivarmakumārakasya
jātādareṇa manasā vacasi prakāmam /
maurkhyaṃ samarpya vigaṇayya kṛtaṃ mayaitat
kāvyaṃ mudā budhavarāḥ pariśodhayantu //50//

Although still suffering, with my mind preoccupied
with the birth of baby Ravivarma,
I have eagerly composed this poem in words,
realizing and setting aside (my) fatuity.[228]
May the best among the learned gladly examine it.

---

[228] This part of the stanza—"realizing and setting aside (my) fatuity"—could be also interpreted as follows: "introducing into the text (my own) stupidity, while at the same time pondering (every word)". Anyway, in both cases it could be a form of a pretence of modesty, adopted to gain the audience's favour. See Kālidāsa's prototypical modest prelude from verses 2–4 of the first book of the *Raghuvaṃśa*.

As was mentioned above, the Kadattanad Royal Family used a prespecified list of names for their male descendants. The name Ravi was one of them. Thus the first male child was named Sankara, the second son in turn Mana, and then Ravi, Udaya or Krishna was put before suffix—varman.

The word *kumāraka* used in the text with regard to Ravi Varma means a little boy. In legal terminology there are several terms to denote a child depending on his age. Thus a boy under five years of age is called *kumāra* (explained as "easily dying"), *śiśu* under eight, *pogaṇḍa* from the 5th till the end of the 9th year and *kiśora* from the 10th until the 16th year of life.

So Ravi Varma was a younger son and a little child under 5, maybe an infant or even a newborn. These are all the pieces of information that can be deduced from the text itself.

I was fortunate enough to have the opportunity to meet several members of the erstwhile rulers of Kadattanad at the beginning of January 2016. Among them was even the great-grandson of the poetess. The knowledge of Lakshmi Tampuratti was quite limited among them. However, in one of their houses an old painting of Lakshmi (Fig. 42, p. 176) was shown to me. The picture shows a traditionally dressed elderly lady. She passed away in 1909 at the age of 64 so it is a portrait over one hundred years old but still the vegetable paint looks quite fresh. The painter has left his signature in the bottom right hand corner of the painting. It was after the success of Raja Ravi Varma (29 April 1848–2 October 1906) of the Kilimanur house as a painter that the practice of signing the paintings by an artist became popular in India. Raja Ravi Varma, an artist uniting European techniques with Indian aesthetics and educated also by the Dutch portraitist Theodor Jenson, is said to have signed his paintings in three types of signature—just his initials: R.V., Ravi Varma or Ravi Varma with the 'V' underlined. The author of the portrait of Lakshmi Tampuratti, T. A. N. Nambisan, put his signature with real dedication: the last letter, *n*, received ornamental squiggle. Nothing can be said about the artist, except for the fact that he followed the path indicated by Raja Ravi Varma. It is not only about the signature, but the arrangement of the scene in the portrait. It reminds one of the portraits of the ladies painted by Raja Ravi Varma. Lakshmi sits on a wooden lathed leg armchair near a small three-legged round table.[229] There is a red cover book on the table, perhaps at that time a costly one.

She wears a traditional dress of a Kerala woman that is mundu neriyatu (Mal. *muṇṭu nēriyatu*). The mundu is a lower garment woven in cotton and coloured white or cream.[230] The border of the mundu is usually thicker, often with a strip of colour woven into it or embroidered. The upper garment, namely melmundu (Mal. *mēlmuṇṭu*) with the same matching border is worn as a kind of shawl. Lakshmi covers her upper body with another mundu or melmundu, not wearing any blouse under it. At that time it was still a common sight to see women not only without any blouse but with naked breasts:

> Covering the bosom formerly signified either a particular location in the Jati-order as Muslim or Christian; or differently done, it could indicate a woman of 'easy virtue'.
> (*Devika 2005: 464–465*)

> The dress reform was a matter of discussion in the late nineteenth and early twentieth century in Kerala. "The well-known 'Breast-Cloth Struggle' of nineteenth-century sought Tiruvitamkoor involved not only the issue of feminine modesty but also struggle around Jati."
> (*Devika 2005: 466*)

Lakshmi Tampuratti, by covering her breasts, was showing her high position but the fact that she is not wearing any blouse is also

[229] We could call this piece of furniture using a word of Indian origin – teapoy if not for its different connotations and complicated history.

[230] Mahatma Gandhi considered white attire of Malayalee women as a symbol of the purity of their mind (Devika 2005: 469).

telling if we take into consideration that it must be the beginning of the twentieth century when her portrait was painted.[231]

Lakshmi wears gold, delicate jewellery: on the little fingers of both hands she has rings with precious stones, and on the third fingers, two rings on each one. She also has two necklaces around her neck, including her tali.[232] Stretched ear lobes show that she certainly wore large and heavy earrings for a long time. She holds a golden rosary in her hand. Gold jewellery was prohibited for groups located lower in the established order, so the gold ornaments reveal her position. The ornaments were painted true to the design and the metal (gold) used to make them. Her hair, probably dyed with henna, is combed in a traditional way.

The portrait speaks also about socio-economic status of the Kadattanad Royal Family at that particular moment, i.e. most probably at the beginning of the 20th century. It was not possible for them to ask Raja Ravi Varma for family portraits. Princes from different Indian states sought his services, as for example the Gaekwads, who offered him a special studio to work in and wanted him to paint the likeness of Maharaja, then Maharani of Baroda and some other works. "Ravi Varma's signature, by then, was an indispensable and widely recognized trademark, denoting the ultimate in luxury (...)" (Neumayer, Schelberger 2005: 1). His clients were very rich, a fact that can be deduced also from the depictions showing them, whereas Lakshmi Rani's dress, jewellery and pieces of Victorian-like furniture on the one hand display the family's affiliation with the local elite aspiring to share European culture but respecting their own tradition and, on the other hand, demonstrating that they were not as rich as Croesus. They were

---

[231] The complex problem of bare-breastedness and the 'history' of the blouse introduction in Kerala is discussed in detail in the engrossing article "The Aesthetic Woman: Re-forming Female Bodies and Minds in Early Twentieth-Century Keralam" (Devika 2005).

[232] Mal. *tāli*—"the centre piece of a neck ornament solemnly tied around the bride's neck as a badge of marriage" (Schildt 2012: 226).

able to hire the best possible painter in the vicinity to commemorate their matriarch and he managed to fulfill his duty accentuating the dignity of the aristocratic lady and showing her social status and education. The index finger of Lakshmi Tampuratti points directly to the book, announcing in this way that it is not merely a prop put on the tripod table but there is a link between the woman and the book declaring her position in the world of men of letters.

Thus the portraits reveal also some stories about the persons depicted on them. There is also the memory of their descendants, if there are any. In line with the family tradition, by writing the poem *Santānagopāla* Lakshmi earned merits. As I was told, Lakshmi's children died just after delivery, all but one—the one, which was born after she had completed the poem. And even though only one of her children survived, she had as many as 18 grandchildren. As it happens, the Brahmin from the Puranic legend lost nine babies.[233] And 9 multiplied by 2 equals 18. So Lakshmi received a doubled number of Brahmin's progeny, though in the next generation and this is remembered by her family.

During my stay in India I visited the Edavalattu Kovilakam or better to say the remains of that old palace. As a result of the land reform the family lost their land and to be able to afford the maintenance of the place, they destroyed the oldest part of it. Luckily, one can still see the delivery room in which Lakshmi herself as well as her children were born. It can be regarded as the meeting place of the two stories, the celestial and earthly ones: the one known from the *Bhāgavata* and the life story of a woman

---

[233] The last child was born alive as the little boy was crying repeatedly, then he disappeared in the sky:

BhP 10.86.38
tataḥ kumāraḥ sañjāto viprapatnyā rudan muhuḥ
sadyo 'darśanam āpede saśarīro vihāyasā //
(*Shastree 1997: 303*)

Fig. 38. Descendants of Lakshmi Tampuratti.

from Kerala. Just like in the case of Trippunitura, the Puranic story mingles with the local context but this time on a different scale—limited to a family circle.

Summing up, as I have already written in my article "The *Santānagopāla* as a Narrative Opening up Intimate Spaces: Lakṣmī Tampurāṭṭi and Her Poem",

> Thanks to collective memory of the members of the Kaṭattanaṭu *rājas* family the story showing what triggered off the compositional process was transmitted to the next century and still is repeated among them. Although extra textual, it should accompany this literary work enlarging and advancing our understanding of it. Without it the interpretation of the last stanza, although disclosing the circumstances, could be different. J. B. Chaudhari in his short *Introduction* to the *Santānagopāla-kāvya* deduced that the poetess was ill, nevertheless out of the affection for Prince Ravivarma, in order to educate him in theological lore, she composed a poem for him (Chaudhari 2001: 27–29).
> (*Sudyka 2018b: 82*)

Obviously, the poem could also serve the didactic purpose as being not only a retelling of the Santānagopāla motif but at the same time providing in its canto 3 some pieces of information about several of Viṣṇu's *avatāras*, concentrating especially on episodes from Kṛṣṇa's life. Nevertheless, without these autobiographical hints the real picture of the situation would not be complete.

To sum up, the story from the *Bhāgavatapurāṇa* was at first adaptively reused in order to create the foundation myth of the Trippunitura temple, then Lakshmi Tampuratti re-used it for her own purposes. To pray for the life of her son was the most important aim but her poem could also serve the boy in the future as the source of knowledge about the Santānagopāla story as well as Kṛṣṇa's tidings. Kṛṣṇa was not only one of the protagonists of the story but the Trippunitura idol is in fact Viṣṇu-Kṛṣṇa as the Protector of Progeny. In such a way Lakshmi provided an extended version of the narrative using her expertise in Puranic lore, and the literary project served her needs well and could be appreciated by its future addressee, namely her son as well as the wider audience. Also Manku Tampuran linked the story as told in the *Bhāgavatapurāṇa* with the Pūrṇatrayīśa myth. However, the degree of adaptiveness[234] is different in all the cases mentioned here.

[234] The adaptiveness of reuse is taken in the sense as proposed by Elisa Freschi and Philip Maas (2017).

Fig. 39. Raja's High School in Purameri.

Fig. 40. Lokanarkavu Temple near Vadakara.

Fig. 41. Edavalattu Kovilakam near Purameri.

Fig. 42. Lakshmi Tampuratti of the Kadattanad Royal Family (1845–1909).

VI. Conclusions

No doubt the persistence of Sanskrit culture in Kerala is also connected with its social organization. Thanks to matriliny the knowledge of Sanskrit could filter from the highest strata of the society i.e. *brahmāṇas* to *śūdras* or even *avarṇa* communities (e.g. *īḻava*). What is particularly important, taking into consideration the subject of the present monograph, Sanskrit education was open to girls. And they took advantage of the possibility for expressing themselves also in this language.

What is worth emphasising, as far as women's Sanskrit education is concerned, is that Kerala poetesses could not repeat the word of Molla Atukuri (early 16th century), who composed *Rāmāyaṇa* in Telugu:

I am no scholar
distinguishing the loanwords
from the native stock.

I know no rule of combination
no large vocabulary.

I am no expert
in composition and illocution,
semantics and style.

Nor do I know
phonetics, case relations,
roots of verbs and figures of speech,
meter and prosody, either.

Untrained though,
in composing poems and epics
in mastering lexicons and rules
I do write poems
by the grace of the famous Lord
Sri Kantha Mallesa.
(Tharu & Lalita (ed.) 1991: 96, 97 transl. by B. V. L. Narayanarow)

Even if spirituality was their real inspiration, as in the case of Molla Atukuri, it was expressed by compositions subjected to Sanskrit grammar and stylistic rules well-known to Kerala poetesses. However, changes taking place in the educational system in Travancore and Cochin first minimized the role of Sanskrit education, and then gradual social and political changes made it possible in the new reality for women from the family of a former royal official (the case of Tottakad Madhavi Amma discussed above) to take places more exposed than the princesses of the Cochin Royal Family.

The authoresses mentioned here lived at a time when it was not easy for women to enter the public space. They could achieve a mastery in the field of literature, science or art, but the knowledge about such a fact was usually restricted to the domestic space. Quite rarely their reputation as good scholars and writers had a chance to reach a wider audience but it cannot be excluded that in their ancestral houses it is still possible to discover the manuscripts providing access to the world of their imagination and life.

The question how their life experiences influenced their own creativity is visible in the poems based on the Santānagopāla plot. At least the two poems attributed to two poetesses, Lakshmi Tampuratti and Manku Tampuran unveil some details concerning their private lives. Manku's poem-dedication entitled the *Mātṛsmaraṇam* can also be added to this category of writings.

These were the rare moments of self-disclosure in women's writings, which are so precious. After all, it is very little what we know about women writing in Sanskrit and sometimes even less about the lives of the authoresses. The *Santānagopāla* plot on which both poems

> are based, shows not only the yearning of the authoresses for a child and portraits the pain of two women who had either lost or desired progeny.
> (*Sudyka 2018b: 82*)

Additionally, the trait clearly visible in these poems is the unconditional faith of both authoresses in God Kṛṣṇa, an *avatāra* of Viṣṇu, who raises the earth from its burden, i.e. makes the *dharaṇi-bhāra* vanish (see *Santānagopālakāvya* of Lakṣmī Tampurāṭṭi, 3.25, 43, 46). This devotion was part and parcel of their everyday life.

That is why hymns to gods dominate in their literary oeuvre. But Kerala's contribution to *stotra* literature, as Kunjunni Raja points out and proves providing the details, is very substantial (Kunjunni Raja 1980: 241, 242). So it is in perfect agreement with this attitude of Kerala poets and their audience that women writing in Sanskrit also went in this direction. If Sanskrit was considered the language of the gods, it would be only proper to eulogize them in their language, especially if the thorough education provided at home supplied a good foundation for Sanskrit grammar and literature.

But it would be perhaps only one side of the matter.

Let us listen to the voice of K. M. Kunhulakshmy Kettilamma (1877–1947), who was a Sanskrit and Malayalam scholar. Her major work in Sanskrit was the *Prārthnāñjali*. She edited a women's magazine *Mahilaratnam* (Devika 2005: 48). Kunhulakshmy Kettilamma writes:

> Literary efforts, especially, are fully dependent on genuine, self-acquired experience. This sort of experience is not available to all women today. The freedom enjoyed by men endows all their endeavours with strength. The restrictions on women's freedom are responsible for the infrequency of their efforts. They must possess at least the social freedom that will permit them to reshape, classify, and refine experience.
> (*Kettilamma 2015; Devika (transl.) 2005: 50*)

Thus, the decision to stay within the well-known world of Hindu mythology perhaps was the easiest one for certain authoresses: familiar, well-known themes and well-defined genres. They could try to write in Malayalam but to conform to the new expectation of the readers was a task beyond the reach of some of them. In this case writing in Sanskrit without the need to express *her-self*[235] seemed safer and still satisfying as one should remember that also well-defined genres and well-known stories allow the innovative approach as many Sanskrit poets have proved.

As the results of my fieldwork show, it can be stated that, it is still possible to find literary works written by women-writers in the 19th and 20th centuries and obtain some data concerning their lives. It seems that the collective memory of members of their families is invaluable as

> (...) it can provide details concerning the life of the poetesses, their education, the writing practices, their contacts which allowed at least some of them to publish their poems; sometimes they indicate what triggered off the compositional process. These points would be extremely interesting for genetic criticism focusing on the reconstruction and analysis of the writing process, as well as for theorists of social editing.[236] The views of old palaces and temples as well as pictures of the authoresses enable us to imagine their lives and this in turn helps in understanding and interpreting their works. Some of these Sanskrit texts were published but these are ephemeral prints, usually sponsored by the families of the poetesses. They are absent from the bookshelves of South Indian libraries, let alone European ones. And if not noticed and preserved, one day they will disappear.

[235] Here I refer to the title of the anthology of J. Devika's choice and translation, containing also the text of Kettilamma.

[236] The ideas of social editing (e.g. Jerome McGann) take into account not only the author but all the other people involved in the process of production (e.g. collaborators, the people who commissioned the work, editors, etc.).

> The Kerala women, who were writing in Sanskrit, authored mainly hymns to their favourite gods. I do not intend to try to convince anyone about the extraordinary values of the literary creativity of the women-writers of Kerala. Nevertheless, there are several high-quality poems amongst their works. These are Lakshmi Tampuratti's *Santānagopāla* and also *Daśakumāracarita* by Ambadevi from Chemprol Kottaram. But far more important than the merits of these poems is the fact that Kerala women's creativity in Sanskrit exists at all. All the authoresses mentioned above proved that they were competent at writing Sanskrit poetry and deserved their own place in a largely male-dominated world of writing. Their literary ocuvre is the best answer to the question articulated by Ikkavamma of the Tottekkat family (Mal. *ikkavāmma toṭṭekkāṭ*, born 1864) in her famous play *Subhadrārjunam* written in Malayalam:
>
> > *Didn't Bhama the dear one to Mallari*
> > *Wage war? And didn't Subhadra drive the chariot?*
> > *Isn't Queen Victoria ruling over this land?*
> > *If women have become experts in all these*
> > *Why then is she deemed incompetent*
> > *for writing poetry alone?*[237] [238]

It is high time we noticed the presence of literature written by women and tried to understand their place not only in the world of Sanskrit culture in Kerala but on a bigger pan-Indian scale. A history of Sanskrit literature that takes account of the presence or absence of women is still to be written.

The first history of Malayalam literature was published in 1881 only. It was the *Malayāḷabhāṣacaritram* by P. Govinda Pillai (Mal.

---

[237] Translated by Nisha M. in her article "Making a Foray into the Uninhabited Grounds of Writing: Thottaikkat Ikkavamma's *Subhadrarjunam*", *Literary Miscellany: An International Journal of Literary Studies* Vol. 4, No.1–2, Jan-Dec 2015.

[238] These conclusions are closing my article "In search of women's Sanskrit writings in Kerala" (Sudyka 2019) which appears simualtaneously with the present book, namely, being a summing-up of my research on that subject.

gōvindappiḷḷa). Contrary to what the title suggests, in reality it is not a history of the Malayalam language but a history of literature written in Malayalam, supplemented with a review of the Sanskrit literature of Kerala. As Udaya Kumar says:

> Literary histories, it must be noted, often perform an important role in giving shape to a literary field not only by determining which texts count as valuable literature but also by establishing relationships of inheritance, transmission and transformation among them. In this sense, literary histories stand in relation to the literary field somewhat like a *parergon* that frames a work, with all the conceptual and methodological complexities that such a connection entails. (*Kumar 2010: 5*)

The first attempts at providing historiography for literary production of Kerala interconnected with many other issues such as the question of community identity (e.g. Brahmin-Nayar relations), defining the literary heritage (i.e. Tamil connections and Sanskrit tradition legacy), social issues (e.g. the case of *sambandham* arrangements discussed vehemently by the social reformers at the turn of the 19th and 20th centuries). Additionally, at this particular time the shift from palm-leaf manuscript culture to the practice of writing on paper as well as the establishing of printing presses took place. One could say that all these completely covered the question about women's participation in the construction of literary heritage of Kerala, but it seems that the time was not yet ripe to formulate it at all. Today the inherited image of the literary past created in the 19th and 20th centuries still points to a very limited presence of women writers although my field studies conducted within limited temporal and spatial dimensions show a more complex picture. After all, Sanskrit culture was part and parcel of their life and identity.

APPENDICES

I. Lakṣmī Tampurāṭṭi

SANTĀNAGOPĀLA[239]

santānagopālakāvyam /
lakṣmīrajñyā viracitam /

atha dvitīyaḥ sargaḥ

atho javān nirjitamārutāśvaṃ
rathaṃ samāruhya rathāṅgapāṇiḥ /
sahasranetrasya sutena sākaṃ
diśaṃ pratīcīṃ prayayau sa devaḥ //1//

tato vyatīte 'drivare tu lokā-
lokābhidhe tatra tamo 'tighoram /
nivārya cakraprabhayā mahatyā
niruddhanetraṃ nijagāda pārtham //2//

vilokyatām āśu vilokanīyaṃ
vilocanāsecanakaṃ janānām /
avarṇyatattanmahimātiśāyi
suparṇaketoḥ padam atyudāram //3//

---

239 The text on the basis of its two previous editions: by Vallauri (1931) and Chaudhari (1940). For the text of the first canto together with its translation, see pp. 146–157.

kadāpi māyāvikṛtiṃ na yāti
bhayādibhāvā api dūrayātāḥ /
prakāśarūpe 'pi ca yatra nityaṃ
paraḥ parānandarasapravāhaḥ //4//

anārjavaṃ yatra bhajaty ajasra-
mahīndrabhogaḥ param eka eva /
virūpatāṃ cāpi khagādhirājo
gadānvitāḥ prāyaśa eva bhaktāḥ //5//

navāmbudaśyāmalakomalāṅgā
gadāmbujādyaṅkitadoścatuṣkāḥ /
śrīvatsapītāmbarakaustubhāḍhyāḥ
śrikāntabhaktā viharanti yasmin //6//

divyāṅganābhiḥ paricaryamāṇā
divyāṃśukāle paribhūṣitāṅgī /
yasmin svayaṃ viśvavimohinī sā
dṛṣṭiprasādaṃ kurute ca lakṣmīḥ //7//

itīrayitvā tarasāvarūḍho
rathād asau pāṇḍusutena sākam /
viveśa pārśvaṃ vihitāñjalī tau
pradṛṣṭavantau ca paraṃ pumāṃsam //8//

phaṇīndraparyaṅkatale śayānaṃ
mahendranīlotpalamecakāṅgam /
kirīṭahārādivibhūṣaṇaugha-
prakṛṣṭanānāmaṇidīpitāśam //9//

lalāṭadeśākalitordhvapuṇḍraṃ
kṛpārasāpūrṇasarojanetram /
suvarṇamīnopamakuṇḍalodyat-
prabhānuliptāmalagaṇḍaśobham //10//

mṛdusmitoddyotimukhendubimbaṃ
galollasatkaustubhaśobhamānam /
caturbhujāsaktagadāriśaṅkha-
saroruhaṃ mañjulavanyamālam //11//

svabhaktavātsalyaviśeṣaśaṃsi-
śrīvatsalakṣmāṅkitavatsadeśam /
anekapaṅkeruhasaṃbhavāṇḍa-
niveśaveśmāyitakukṣideśam //12//

pītāmbarācchāditapīvaroruṃ
pāpāndhakārāruṇapādapadmam /
nakhenduvidhvastasamastabhakta-
janāntarasthāyimahāndhakāram //13//

sanatkumārādimunīndramukhyaiḥ
sanandamukhyair api pāriṣadyaiḥ /
surāsurādyair api mūrtimadbhir
nijāyudhaiḥ santatam īḍyamānam //14//

tadīyarūpāpahṛtākṣipadmāv
amū parānandapayodhimagnau
skhaladgirā tuṣṭuvatus tadānīṃ
jagadguruṃ pāṇḍavavāsudevau //15//

namo namas te nalinekṣaṇāya
navāmbudaśyāmakalevarāya /
padāravindapraṇatākhilārtha-
pradānasantānamahīruhāya //16//

namo 'dvitīyāya sadāstu tubhyaṃ
purāṇapuṃse prakṛteḥ parasmai /
prapañcasargasthitināśakartre
viriñcaviṣṇvīśavapurdharāya //17//

yogīśvarāntarnilayāya dhāmne
bodhasvarūpāya nirañjanāya /
buddhīndriyaprāṇavilakṣaṇāya
satyātmakāyāstu namo namas te //18//

sarvātmane sarvavilakṣaṇāya
sarvāntarasthāya sadāśivāya /
saccitparānandamayāya śuddha-
tattvasvarūpāya namo namas te //19//

yasmād idaṃ viśvam udeti sarvaṃ
yasmin pratiṣṭhāṃ labhate punas tat /
yatraiva yāti pralayaṃ ca tasmai
tubhyaṃ namo 'stv adbhutavaibhavāya //20//

vidhāya māyāpratibimbitas tvaṃ
prapañcam etan mahadāditattvaiḥ /
saṃhṛtya bhūyaḥ kila kālaśaktyā
prakāśase tvaṃ hi mahāprakāśaḥ //21//

vidhāya līlānilayaṃ kiśoraḥ
praviśya cāntaḥ suciraṃ vihṛtya /
vināśayaty eva punas tu sarvaṃ
tathaiva nātha tvam idaṃ ca viśvam //22//

māyāmaye saṃsṛtisāgare 'smin
kāyātmabuddhyā suciraṃ bhramantaḥ /
tavaiva saṃprāpya padābjapotaṃ
taranti taṃ goṣpadavan mathantaḥ //23//

bhavinniketabhramaṇe sadā me
dhṛtābhilāṣau caraṇau bhavetām /
karau bhavatpādasarojapūjā-
ratau śrutī tvaccaritaśrutau ca //24//

mukunda te mūrtivilokanotke
vilocane cāpi sadā bhavetām /
ghrāṇaṃ ca yuṣmatpadapadmapuṣpa-
ghrāṇotsukaṃ santatam astu viṣṇo //25//

tavāvatārādikathāprasaṅga-
ratā sadā syād rasanāsmadīyā /
mūrdhā praṇāmapravaṇo 'stu nityaṃ
dhyāne mano me madhudānavāre //26//

iti stuto 'yaṃ sarasīruhākṣaḥ
smitāmṛtāsaktamukhāravindaḥ /
kṛpārasāpūrṇakaṭākṣapataiḥ
praharṣayann āha pumān purāṇaḥ //27//

kim adya bhoḥ kṛṣṇadhanañjayau vām
anāhataṃ kṣemam udāravīryau /
nivedyatāṃ svāgatam apy aho yan
madantike 'py āgamane nidānam //28//

pṛṣṭo bataivaṃ puruṣottamena
pracchādya tāvan nijasarvavittvam /
vijñāpayāmāsa yadūdvaho 'smai
vijñānarūpāya kṛtapraṇāmaḥ //29//

nivedanīyaṃ tvayi sarvavedin
na vidyate kiñcana devadeva /
divākarasyātra tamonirodhaḥ
prakāśarūpasya bhavet kathaṃ vā //30//

tathāpi lokānukṛtis taveyaṃ
padāśritānugrahahetur eva /
pipāsutā hanta payodharāṇāṃ
nijāśrayāṇām iva cātakānām //31//

dvijasya kasyāpi tanūbhavasya
prapālane sādhu kṛtapratijñaḥ /
dhanañjayo 'yaṃ viphalaprayatnaḥ
paratra sarvatra vicitya jātaḥ //32//

bhavatprasāde sati durlabhaṃ kiṃ
bhavej janasyeti vicintya nātha /
anena sākaṃ bhavataḥ sakāśaṃ
samāgato 'smy adya saroruhākṣa //33//

ayi prapannārtihara prasanno
bhaveti bhūyo 'pi kṛtapraṇāmaḥ /
sudhām ivāmāndakṛpārasārdro
jagāda vācaṃ jagatāṃ śaraṇyaḥ //34//

kartuṃ yuvām adya madaṃśabhūtāv
anekahiṃsājanitāghamuktau /
padāvalokān mama te kumārā
dvijottamasyātra mayeiva nītāḥ //35//

ciraṃ pṛthivyāṃ kuśalaṃ bhajantau
padaṃ samāgacchatam etad evam /
nayetam etān api vipraputrān
pratiśrutaṃ tat tu bhavatv abandhyam //36//

iti madhuripuṇā kṛtābhyanujñau
yaduvarapāṇḍusutāv atiprahṛṣṭau
padasarasijayor nipatya bhūyo
dvijatanyaiś ca tataḥ pratasthivāṃsau //37//

iti dvitīyaḥ sargaḥ //

atha tṛtīyaḥ sargaḥ /

atha tadā harilokavilokanād
uditatattvadhiyā sa dhanañjayaḥ /
kṛtaharistutir astamado 'viśad
dvijagṛhe jagṛhe ca parāṃ mudam //1//

sutavināśaviṣādavimūrcchitaṃ
drutam upetya tadā dvijasattamam /
saha nipatya pade vijayo 'bravīt
sa hariṇā hariṇāṃkakulāṃkuraḥ //2//

dvijavara praṇato 'smi dhanañjayas
tava padābjayuge sahabālakaḥ /
anugṛhāṇa viṣādam aśeṣayan
dayitayāyi tayātiśucārtayā //3//

daśamanandanapālanam eva te
dvijakulendra mayā tu purāśrutam /
bata paraṃ madhuvairikṛpābalād
anihatān iha tān daśa cānayam //4//

iti nipīya tadīyavaco'mṛtaṃ
gurutarapramadākulamānasaḥ /
kṣaṇam abhūt pratipattivimūḍhadhīr
dvijavaro javarodhivikārataḥ //5//

samupaguhya dṛḍhaṃ punar āśu taṃ
śirasi cāpy abhicumbya muhur muhuḥ /
pramadavāṣpajalāny abhivarṣatā
sa jagade jagadekadhanurdharaḥ //6//

ayi dhanañjaya jīva ciraṃ sukhī
sutadhanādisamastasamṛddhimān /
pṛthu yaśaś ca bhujābalam akṣataṃ
bhavatu te 'vatu tena mahīṃ bhavān //7//

samadhikādhikamodavidhāyinaḥ
pratividhānam aho na jagattraye /
kim adhikaṃ bata dātum idaṃ jagad
vijaya te jayate bhujavikramaiḥ //8//

iha tu dīnaparāyaṇa sarvadā
yadupatiḥ sa dadātu hitaṃ tava /
nijavayovilaye 'pi ca yoginām
asulabhaṃ sulabhaṃ padamastu tat //9//

iti vitirya tadāśiṣam agrato
madhuripuṃ ca samīkṣva mahīsuraḥ /
sudṛḍhabhaktiyutaḥ praṇipatya taṃ
param udāram udāram athāstuvat //10//

jaya hare jaya deva jagatpate
yadukulāmbudhipūrṇaniśākara /
ayam ahaṃ praṇato 'smi ramāpate
tava padeva padekasamāśrayama //11//

ahaha viśvavimohanaśīlayā
tava paraṃ jagadīśvara māyayā /
hatadhiyaḥ kalayanti mahātmatāṃ
manasi te na sitetarakarmabhiḥ //12//

tad iha me nikhilām aparādhitāṃ
sutavināśaśucā vacasā kṛtām /
sadayam adya sahasva kṛpāṃ vinā
tribhuvane bhuvaneśvara kā gatiḥ //13//

yad iha dustarasaṃsṛtisāgare
sudṛḍhavāsanayā tu nimajjataḥ /
agham aho pratijanma samarjitaṃ
tvam adhunā madhunāśana nāśaya //14//

dṛdhatarā tvayi bhaktir aharniśaṃ
bhavatu me bhavatāpavināśinī /
apanayasva hṛdo 'py avivekitāṃ
karuṇayāruṇayā nayanaśriyā //15//

satatam eva jagat parirakṣituṃ
nikhilam apy avatāraśatair alam /
kṛtadhiyas tava sā prathitā kṛpā
bhuvi tathā vitathām iha mā kṛthāḥ //16//

divibhuvā hayakaṇṭha iti prathāṃ
gatavatāpahṛte nigamotkare /
tava tu tatra dhṛtā sakalāpadāṃ
śamakarī makarīśatanuḥ purā //17//

pramathite tu purā payasāṃ nidhau
militasarvasurāsurasañcayaiḥ /
vipulakacchaparūpam adhogataṃ
mahidharaṃ hi dharantam upāsmahe //18//

śaraṇam astu sa me kiṭirūpadhṛg
jalanidhāv asureṇa nimajjitā /
kṣitir iyaṃ bata yena samuddhṛtā
sa ca raṇe caraṇena hato ripuḥ //19//

ditisutaṃ nijabhaktasuradruhaṃ
kaśipum ādihiraṇyapadaṃ nakhaiḥ /
naramṛgendravapur hatavān bhavān
vasatu me sa tu medhyatamo hṛdi //20//

tam aham indrasahodaram āśraye
tripadamātramitāṃ tu jagattrayīm /
balikarād apahṛtya ca yaḥ purā
maghavate 'ghavate pradadau mudā //21//

hṛdi karomy aniśaṃ jamadagnijaṃ
dvijakulāpakṛtau niratā nṛpāḥ /
sapadi yasya paraśvadhanāmake
hutavahe tava he śalabhāḥ kṛtāḥ //22//

surajanārthanayā dinakṛtkule
daśarathātmajatāṃ samupetya taḥ /
daśamukhaṃ tu jaghāna jagaddruhaṃ
sa bhava me bhavameduratāpahā //23//

sitapayodharacārutarākṛtir
vidhṛtanīlapaṭo musalāyudhaḥ /
iha ca samprati naḥ śaraṇaṃ bhavāñ
chamayatām ayatām agham ulvaṇam //24//

kaliyuge 'ntam upeṣyati kalkinaḥ
khalajanān akhilāṃś ca vibhetsyataḥ /
tava padābjayugaṃ tad idaṃ manaḥ
smarati me ratim ekatamāṃ vahat //25//

yam iha yādavavaṃśasamudbhavaṃ
dharaṇibhāravināśavidhitsayā /
sapadi kaṃsabhayena pitānayad
vrajapade 'ja padena taran nadīm //26//

sapadi tatra ca kaṃsaniyojitā
viṣaviliptakucaṃ diśatī tava /
niśicarī bata yena hi pūtanā
sunihatā nihatāmitabālakā //27//

tava vadhāya punaś ca samāgatāḥ
śakaṭavātamukhā bahavo 'surāḥ /
makhabhujām aniśaṃ ca hitaiṣiṇā
vidalitā dalitārjunabhūruhā //28//

nikhilagopavadhūnilayād api
svajananī navanītapayomuṣaḥ /
niyamanaṃ tu kathañcid ulūkhale
kṛtavatī tava tīvraruṣākulā //29//

sakalagopakumārakasaṃkule
bhavati gośiśupālanalolupe /
kamalabhūr api yasya tu māyayā
paramayāram ayād iha vismayam //30//

svaviṣadūṣitasūryasutājalaṃ
vimadayan phaṇināyakam āśu yaḥ /
surajanena sumair abhivarṣataḥ
stutavatā tava tāṇḍavacāturīm //31//

jalavihāravidhau yamunātaḍe
nihitamaṃśukasañjayamāharan /
brajavadhūrakarostrapayāturāḥ
samadanā madanādhikamohanaḥ //32//

ruṣitavāsavavṛṣṭibhayaṃ vraje
praśamayan svakaroddhṛtaparvataḥ /
gatamadena śacīpatinā punar
divibhavair vibhavaiḥ samapūji yaḥ //33//

muralikāsvanamohitamānasair
vrajavadhūnivahaiḥ saha yo bhavān /
bahutanur bahudhāpi ca khelanaṃ
vyatanutātanutāpabharākulaiḥ //34//

kalayatā bahularddhim aho vraje
gatavatāpi punar madhurāpurīm /
vadhujanā nayanāñcalaśṛṅkhalā-
vigalitā galitānyarasāḥ kṛtāḥ //35//

ṛjutanūm anulepanadāyinīm
atha vidhāya sudāmamukharcitaḥ /
rajakamallamukhaiḥ saha mātulaṃ
niravadhīr avadhīritasatpatham //36//

upanayād atha śikṣitasatkalo
mṛtatanūbhavajīvanadakṣiṇaḥ /
anumataḥ prayayau ca nijāṃ purīṃ
svaguruṇā guruṇā pramadena yaḥ //37//

bahutaraṃ tu jarāsutadormadaṃ
śithilayan mucukundagatipradaḥ /
jalanidhāv akarod atidurgamām
asuhṛdāṃ suhṛdāṃ sugamāṃ purīm //38//

viditabhīṣmasutāhṛdayas tu yo
dvijakumāragirāśritakuṇḍinaḥ /
priyatamāṃ ca jahāra virodhino
viśikhayañ śikhayann api rukmiṇam //39//

dinakarāptamaṇer api yādavād
bhavati durvacanāc cakitātmanaḥ /
api varād api (?) labdhasutas tayor
urubhayor ubhayoḥ karam agrahīḥ //40//

kṛtakalindasutākarapīḍanaḥ
sapadi madramahīśasutādikāḥ /
karabalāt parigṛhya ca bālikās
tv aramayo ramayopamitāṃgakāḥ //41//

narakadaityaniyantritasundarī-
janam aho pariṇītavataḥ punaḥ /
suramunipravarāya nidarśita-
svamahimā mahimāpi ca yasya te //42//

atha yudhiṣṭhirayajñasabhājana-
praruṣitasya tu cedimahīśituḥ /
nidhanam āśu vidhāya yayau punar
yajanato janatoṣakaro bhavān //43//

api ca sālvamukhān akhilān ahann
atha dhanañjayasārathitāṃ gataḥ /
dharaṇibhāraharaḥ sukham āvasaḥ
svasadane sadanekajanāśrite //44//

giriśasevakabāṇamadāpahā
nṛgamahīśavimokṣavidhāyinī /
drupadajāṃbarabhaṃgasamīratās
upagatāpagatāriṣu yatkṛpā //45//

nijakalatrahitāya dhanārthinaṃ
priyasakhaṃ tu kucelamahīsuram /
akṛta yaḥ pṛthukāśanato 'dhikaṃ
sudhanado dhanadopamamāśu tam //46//

sa tvaṃ sattvatanuḥ samastakalayā purṇo 'vatirṇaḥ kule
vṛṣṇīnām iha bhūmibhāraharaṇe yo 'bhyarthito vedhasā /
nārīnāṃ nayanāmṛtāyitavapuś caidyādidiṣṭāntakṛd
bhaktānām akhilārthakalpakataruḥ kṛṣṇaidhi naḥ śreyase //47//

iti kṣiti surottamapriyam anena saṃpādayan
surādhipasutena ca pramadabhārapūrṇātmanā /
sametya nijamandiraṃ saha kalatraputrādibhiḥ
samṛddhayaśasā sukhaṃ suciram atra reme hariḥ //48//

vihārair ity ādyair jagad akhilam ānandabharitaṃ
vitanvan bhaktānāṃ paramagatidānaikanirataḥ /
aśeṣāghadhvāntapraśamanadineśāyitaguṇaḥ
sa kṛṣṇaḥ kalyāṇaṃ kalayatu sadā vo bahutaram //49//

rogārtayā 'pi ravivarmakumārakasya
jātādareṇa manasā vacasi prakāmam /
maurkhyaṃ samarpya vigaṇayya kṛtaṃ mayaitat
kāvyaṃ mudā budhavarāḥ pariśodhayantu //50//

iti tṛtīyaḥ sargaḥ //3//
samāptaṃ cedaṃ kāvyam /

II. Maṅku Tampurāṭṭi

SANTĀNAGOPĀLA[240]

santānagopālam //

śrī maṅkuttampurān maṅgalālayam /

vande gajānanaṃ devaṃ vāṇīṃ vīṇāvinodinīm /
haraṃ gurūn hṛdantasthaṃ paradaivaṃ hariṃ param //1//

kasyacid dvijamukhyasya dvārakāpuravāsinaḥ /
jāto bhūsparśamātreṇa mṛtaḥ putro babhūva hā //2//

mṛtaṃ putram athādāya sabhāyāṃ nyasya bhūsuraḥ /
vilalāpātiduḥkhārtaḥ kṛṣṇaṃ nirbhatsya nirgataḥ //3//

evam aṣṭa mṛtān bālān tatra nikṣipya sa dvijaḥ /
duḥkhito 'tīva vilapan bhūyas svagṛham āgataḥ //4//

navamaṃ mṛtam ānīya sabhādvāri nidhāya saḥ /
vilapantaṃ yathāpūrvaṃ vijayo vākyam abravīt //5//

naiveme kṣatriyā brahman daśamaṃ pālayāmy aham /
noced vahniṃ pravekṣyāmi sadhanvā nātra saṃśayaḥ //6//

tac churtvā phalgunaṃ prāha vipro bāliśatā hy asau /
saṅkarṣaṇo vāsudevaḥ pradyumnas tatsuto 'pi yat //7//

nāśakam[241] tat sādhayāmīty akaroc chapathaṃ katham /
viśvāsārhan na me kiñcid vacanaṃ bhavati kvacit //8//

tadākarṇyārjunaḥ prāha nāhaṃ saṅkarṣaṇādikaḥ /
gāṇḍīvadhanvā pārtho 'haṃ yadi te śrotram āgataḥ //9//

---

[240] The text on the basis of the copy from the private archive of Chandravali Thampuran. Published in the anthology I was not able to trace.

[241] Em. t.

toṣayitvā raṇe śaṃbhuṃ labdhaṃ pāśupataṃ mayā /
tad vīryeṇāham āneṣye bālakam te 'ntakād api //10//

evam āśvāsito vipraḥ pārthenātha gṛhaṃ gataḥ /
tatra gatvātiduḥkhārtāṃ patnīṃ vīkṣya suduḥkhitaḥ //11//

śanair āśvāsayāmāsa pārthavīryapraśaṃsayā /
punar garbham adhāt patnī viprasya daśamaṃ satī //12//

phalgunaṃ prārthayāmāsa bālarakṣām atha dvijaḥ /
tathethety uktvā śaraiḥ kṛtvā pañjaraṃ dvāri saṃsthitaḥ //13//

tadā rudan gato bālo hāhākāro mahān abhūt /
nāhaṃ saṅkarṣaṇetyādi sadarpaklībakatthanam //14//

mayājñānād viśvasitaṃ sadhanvā vahnim āviśa /
evaṃ vipravacaḥ śrutvā vijayo 'tha yamālayam //15//

gatvābravīd ihānīto bālako me pradīyatam /
dvārakāyāṃ viprapatnyās suto jāto mṛtas tadā //16//

taṃ vicityāham āyātaḥ tatrālabdhvā divaṃ gataḥ
tatrāpy adṛṣṭvā dikmālamandireṣv akhileṣv api //17//

vicityālabdhabālo 'sau mahīṃ prāpa tato 'nalam /
prajvālya manasā kṛṣṇaṃ sañcintyāgnau kalevaram //18//

dagdhukāmam athāgatya kṛṣṇo jiṣṇuṃ nyavārayat /
sakhe tvayā pratijñātam akhilaṃ sādhayām[242]y aham //19//

ity uktvā dārukānītaṃ ratham āruhya sārjunaḥ /
pratīcīm diśam uddiśya yayau kṛṣṇo vihāyasā //20//

saptasindhugiridvīpān atītya samahārathaḥ /
lokālokam atikramya gacchann andham tamo 'viśat //21//

phalgunaś cātisaṃbhrāntaḥ kim etad iti cāvidan /
bhagavān atha tadvīkṣya sahasrāraṃ sudarśanam //22//

[242] Em. v.

cakraṃ saṃsmārāvirabhūt puro mārgapradarśakaḥ /
sahasrāṃśusahasrābhaḥ sahasrākṣasutas tadā //23//

nayane tarasācchādya sthitaḥ tikṣṇaprabhāsaḥ /
tad vikṣya sahasā so 'bhūt somakoṭisamaprabhaḥ //24//

tatormimālaṃ salilaṃ praviṣṭo
dadarśa tatrādbhutam uttamottamam /
sthānaṃ maṇisthūṇavirājamānaṃ
śeṣaṃ ca śīrṣasthamaṇipradīptam //25//

tadbhogasaṃsthaṃ puruṣottamaṃ ca
kirīṭahārādivibhūṣitāṅgam /
pītāmbaraṃ padmaviśālanetraṃ
kālāmbudābhaṃ kamanīyarūpam //26//

sunandanandādimahānubhāvaiś
cakrādibhir mūrtidharaiḥ parītam /
dadarśa kṛṣṇas saha jiṣṇunā ca
nanāma bhaktyā tam ananyarūpam //27//

uvāca kṛṣṇaṃ harir evam etān
ānītavān vipravarātmajātān /
sandarśanārthaṃ yuvayos tarīyān
nītvātha viprāya ca tān dadātu //28//

tatheti kṛṣṇas saha jiṣṇunā tān
ānīya viprāya dadau kumārān /
vipro 'py aśeṣāśiṣam arjunāya
datvā mudaṃ prāpa nanāma kṛṣṇam //29//

phalguno hariṇā dattaṃ bimbam ādāya sādaram /
pūrṇatrayīśapure sthāpya paraṃ harṣam avāptavān //30//

List of Illustrations

Figures[1]

[1] All the photos are taken by the author.

Bibliography

Primary sources

Amba Tampuratti of Punjar

—. *Rāmāyaṇastuti*, Gayathri Publications Pvt. Ltd., Poonjar, 2001.

—. *Bhaktisagaram*, Pentograph Publications India, Thiruvananthapuram, 2018.

Ambadevi Tampuratti of Chemprol of Kottaram

Daśakumāracarita. A manuscript in the possesion of C. Raja Raja Varma.

Asvati Tirunal Rama Varma

Santānagopāla-Prabandha. with the Commentary of P. Govindaru Nampurippad. Irinjalakkuda: Tharaṇanalloor Nedumpilli Mana, 1954.

Balarama Varma

Bālarāmabharatam of Śrī Bālarāma Varma Vanci Maharaja. K. Sāmbaśiva Śāstrī (ed.). Trivandrum: Government Press, 1935.

Bhamaha

Kāvyālaṅkāra of Bhāmaha. P. V. Naganatha Sastry (ed. and transl.). Delhi: Motilal Banarsidass Publishers, 1991.

Bhāgavatapurāṇa

BhP=*The Bhāgavata. Critical Edition*. Shastree, K. K. (ed.).

Skandha X. Vol. 4. Ahmadabad: B. J. Institute of Learning and Research, 1997.

Bhoja
Śṛṅgāraprakāśa. Bhojarāja Granthamālā. 1. R. S. Saini (ed.). Delhi: Nag Publishers, 2001.

Dandin
—. *Avantisundarī*, Śūranāḍ Kuñjan Pilla (ed.). Trivandrum, 1954.
—. *Dasakumaracharita of Daṇḍin, Text with Sanskrit Commentary, Various Readings, A Literal English Translation, Explanatory and Critical Notes, and an Exhaustive Introduction*, by M. R. Kale. Delhi: Motilal Banarsidass,1986.

Chandumenon, O.
Indulekha. A. Devasia (transl.). New Delhi: Oxford University Press, 2013.

Chandravali Tampuran (ed.). *Pāhi Pūrṇatrayīśa!* Thiruvananthapuram: Akshara Offset, 2009.

Devaki Nilayamgode
Antharjanam: Memoirs of a Namboodiri Woman. I. Menon and R. P. Menon (transl.). New Delhi: Oxford University Press, 2011.

Devaraja Kavi
The Bālamārtāṇḍavijayam of Devarāja Kavi. K. Sāmbhaśiva Sāstri (ed.). Tivandrum Sanskrit. No. 108. Trivandrum: Government Press, 1930.

Kerala Varma Valiya Koyil Tampuran
The Peacock Messenger: Mayūradūtam with an English Translation by K. Narayana Pillai. Trivandrum: P. K. Narayana Pillai, 1984.

Koccammini Tampuran
Pūrṇatrayīśa mama dehi karāvalambam, Vande devam jagad-

gurum. In: Chandravali Thampuran (ed.). *Pāhi Pūrṇatrayīśa!* Thiruvananthapuram: Akshara Offset, 2009: 214–216.

Lakshmi Tampuratti

SGK= *Santānagopāla-kāvya.* In:

—. J. B. Chaudhari. 2001. *The Contribution of Women to Sanskrit Literature.* Vol. 2. Sanskrit Poetesses. New Delhi: Cosmo Publications 49–85.

—. M. Vallauri. Il "Saṁtanagopālakāvya" di Lakṣmīrājñī. *Memorie della R. Accademia nazionale dei Lincei. Classe di scienze morali, storiche e filologiche.* Vol. 4. Roma: G. Bardi, 1931.

Manku Tampuran

—. *Stutiratnamālā.* Pūrṇavedapuri: Rājā Prasū, 1964.

—. *Śrīpūrṇatrayīśasuprabhāta.* In: Chandravali Thampuran (ed.). *Pāhi Pūrṇatrayīśa*, Thiruvananthapuram: Akshara Offset, 2009: 198–200.

—. *Santānagopāla.* (From the private archive of Chandravali Thampuran).

Matampu Kunhukuttan

Outcaste. Vasanthi Sankaranarayanan (transl.). New Delhi: Aleph, 2019.

Melpputtur Narayana Bhatta

Ajamilamokṣaprabandha of Nārāyaṇa Bhaṭṭa. Pandit V. Venkaṭarāma Śarmā Śāstrī (ed.). In: *Bulletin of the School of Oriental Studies* 4(2): 295–300. https://doi.org/10.1017/s0041977x00089217.

Nilakantha Dikshita

Rāmāyaṇasaṃgraha. In: *Oeuvres Poétiques de Nīlakaṇṭha Dīkṣita.* Text, traduction et notes par Pierre-Sylvain Filliozat. Pondichéry: Institut Français D'Indologie, 1967.

Ramapanivada

Śārikasandeśa of Rāmapāṇivāda. Edited with a Sanskrit Commentary and a Critical Study by C. M. Nilakandhan, Delhi: Nag Publishers, 1987.

Subhadra (Ikku Amma Tampuran)
—. *Pūrṇatrayīśastotram*. In: *Journal of the Kerala University Oriental Manuscripts Library*, 1965, 14(4): 1–10.
—. *Saubhadrastavam*, *Śrīṃadbhāgavatasaṃgraham*, *Prārthanāślokas*, *Devīmāhātmyāṣṭaka*, *Śrīpūrṇatrayīśakeśādipādam*. In: Chandravali Thampuran (ed.). *Pāhi Pūrṇatrayīśa!*. Thiruvananthapuram: Akshara Offset, 2009: 152–168.

Sukumara
Kiḷimānūr Sethu Tampurāṭṭi, (transl.) 2011. Sukumāra. *Śrīkṛṣṇavilāsam*. Kochi: Kurukshetra Prakasan.

Swami Vivekananda
The Complete Works of Swami Vivekananda. Vol. 7. Calcutta: Advaita Ashrama, 1989.

Secondary literature

Antony, T. 2013. Women's Education: A Reading of Early Malayalam Magazines. In: *Artha - Journal of Social Sciences* 12(3): 19–42. https://doi.org/10.12724/ajss.26.2.

Bayly, S. 1984. Hindu Kingship and the Origin of Community: Religion, State and Society in Kerala, 1750–1850. In: *Modern Asian Studies* 18(2): 177–213. https://doi.org/10.1017/s0026749x00014402.

Bushell, S. 2005. Intention Revisited: Towards an Anglo-American "Genetic Criticism". In: *Text* 17: 55–91.

Branfoot, C. 2000. Approaching the Temple in Nayaka-Period Madurai: The Kūṭal Aḻakar Temple. In: *Artibus Asiae* 60(2): 197–221. https://doi.org/10.2307/3249918.

Bronner, Y. 2012. A Question of Priority: Revisiting the Bhāmaha-Daṇḍin Debate. In: *Journal of Indian Philosophy* 40(1): 67–118. https://doi.org/10.1007/s10781-011-9128-x.

Buchanan, 1807. *Journey from Madras through the Countries of Mysore, Canara, and Malabar Performed under the Order of the Most Noble Marquis Wellesley, Governor General of India for the Express Purpose of Investigation the State of Agriculture, Arts, and Commerce; the Religion, Manners, and Customs; the History Natural and Civil, and Antiquities, in the Dominions of the Rajah of Mysore, and the Countries Acquired by the Honourable East India Company, in the Late and Former Wars, from Tippoo Sultaun.* London: W. Bulmer and CO. Cleveland Row.

Cielas, H. 2016. The Implementation of Pan-Indian Form on Keralan Ground. A. R. Rajaraja Varma's Citranakṣatramālā. In: *Cracow Indological Studies* 18: 241–264. https://doi.org/10.12797/cis.18.2016.18.10.

Champakalakshmi, R., et al. 2002. *State and Society in Premodern South India.* Thrissur: Cosmobooks.

Chaudhari, J. B. 2001. *The Contribution of Women to Sanskrit Literature.* Vol. 2. *Sanskrit Poetesses.* New Delhi: Cosmo Publications.

Cherian, P. J. (ed.). 1999. *Essays of the Cultural Formation of Kerala. Literature, Art, Architecture, Music, Theatre and Cinema.* Kerala state gazetteer. Vol. 4. Pt. 2. Thiruvananthapuram: Kerala State Gazetteers Department.

Dalmia, V. 1999. *The Nationalization of Hindu Traditions. Bhāratendu Hariśchandra and Nineteenth-Century Banaras.* New Delhi: Oxford University Press.

Datta, A. (ed.). 1988. *Encyclopaedia of Indian Literature: Devraj to Jyoti.* Vol. 2, New Delhi: Sahitya Akademi.

Davies, F. S. 1923. *Cochin. British Indian.* London: Simpkin, Marshall, Hamilton, Kent Co. Ltd.

Davis Jr., D. R. 2013. Matrilineal Adoption, Inheritance Law, and Rites for the Dead among Hindus in Medieval Kerala. In: *Religion and Identity in South Asia and Beyond. Esseys in Honour of Patrick Olivelle.* S. E. Lindquist (ed.). London–New York–Delhi: Anthem Press: 147–164.

De Lannoy, M. 1997. *The Kulasekhara Perumals of Travancore. History and State Formation in Travancore from 1671 to 1758.* Leiden: Research School CNWS, School of Asian, African, and Amerindian Studies.

Devadevan, M. V. 2014. Changes in Land Relations during the Decline of the Cera State. In: Kesavan Veluthat, Donald R. Davis, Jr. (ed.). Irreverent History. Essays for M.G.S. Narayanan, Delhi: Primus Books: 53-80.

Devika, J. 2005. *The Aesthetic Woman: Re-forming Female Bodies and Minds in Early Twentieth-Century Keralam.* In: *Modern Asian Studies* 39(2): 461–487. https://doi.org/10.1017/s0026749x04001519.

—. 2007. *En-gendering Individuals. The Language of Re-forming in Early Twentieth Century Keralam.* New Delhi: Orient Longman.

—. (ed. and transl.). 2005. *Her-self. Early Writings on Gender by Malayalee Women 1898–1938.* Kolkata: Stree.

Eapen, M. and P. Kodoth. 2002. *Family Structure, Women's Education and Works: Re-examining the High Status of Women in Kerala.* Working Paper Series 341. Thiruvananthapuram: Centre for Development Studies.

Easwaran Nampoothiry, E. 1972. *Sanskrit Literature of Kerala. An Index of Authors with Their Works.* Trivandrum: College Book House.

—. 1983. *Bālarāmabharatam. A Critique on Dance and Drama.* Trivandrum: Keralasanskritam Publications.

Fawcett, F. 1901. *Nâyars of Malabar.* Madras Government Museum Bulletin. Anthropology. Vol. 3. No. 3. Madras: Government Press.

Freeman, R. 2003. Genre and Society: The Literary Culture of Premodern Kerala. In: S. Pollock (ed.). *Literary Cultures in History. Reconstructions from South Asia*, Berkeley: University of California Press: 437–500.

Frenz, M. 2003. *From Contact to Conquest. Transition to British Rule in Malabar, 1790–1805.* New Delhi: Oxford University Press.

Freschi, E., Maas, P. 2017. Introduction: Conceptual Reflections on Adaptive Reuse. In: E. Freschi and P. Maas (eds). *Adaptive Reuse. Aspects of Creativity in South Asian Cultural History.* Wiesbaden: Harrassowitz Verlag.

Fuller, C. J. 1976. *The Nayars Today.* Cambridge: Cambridge University Press.

Galewicz, C. 2002–2003. Testing Chanting Skills at Kaṭavallur Anyōnyam. In: *Cracow Indological Studies* 4/5: 211–225.

—. 2003. A Keen Eye on Details. Reviving Ritual Perfection in Trichur Somayaga. In: *Bulletin d'Études Indiennes* 21(1): 239–253.

—. 2004. *Kaṭavallur Anyōnyam: A Competition in Vedic Chanting?* In: A. Griffiths and J. E. M. Houben (eds). *The Vedas. Texts, Language Ritual. Proceedings of the Third International Vedic Workshop, Leiden 2002.* Groningen: Egbert Forsten: 361–384.

—. 2015. *Żyjace biblioteki Indii. Rygweda braminów Nambudiri.* Kraków: Wydawnictwo Uniwersytetu Jagiellońskiego.

—. 2019. *Kingdoms of Memory. Empires of Ink.The Veda and the Print Cultures of Colonial India*. Kraków: Wydawnictwo Uniwersytetu Jagiellońskiego (forthcoming).

Ganesh, K. N. 2002. Land Rights and Political Structure in Medieval Vēnāṭu. In: R. Champakalakshmi et al. (ed.). *State and Society in Pre-modern South India*. Thrissur: Cosmobooks: 144–171.

Ganesh, K. N. 2014. From Nadu to Swarupam: Political Authority in Southern Kerala from the Tenth to the Thirteenth Centuries. In: K. Veluthat and D. R. Davis Jr. (eds). *Irreverent History. Essays for M.G.S. Narayanan*, Delhi: Primus Books: 33–52.

Gough, E. K. 1954. *The Traditional Kinship System of the Nayars of Malabar*. Cambridge: Harvard University.

George, K. M. 1968. *A Survey of Malayalam Literature*. London: Asia Publishing House.

Gerow, E. 1971. *A Glossary of Indian Figures of Speech*. The Hague: Paris: Mouton.

Gouri Lakshmi Bayi, A. T. 2000. *Sree Padmanabha Swamy Temple*. Mumbai: Bharatiya Vidya Bhavan.

Govinda Varma Raja, E. K. 2007. *The King without a Crown*. Calicut: Kamala Press.

Hamilton, A. 1995. *A New Account of the East-Indies: Trading and Travelling, by Sea and Land, to Most of the Countries and Islands of Commerce and Navigation, between the Cape of Good-Hope and the Island of Japan; Being the Observations and Remarks of Alexander Hamilton from the Year 1688 to 1723*. 2 Vols. New Delhi: Asian Educational Services.

Heston, M. B. 1996. *The Nexus of Divine and Earthly Rule: Padmanabhapuram Palace and Traditions of Architecture and Kingship in South Asia*. In: *Ars Orientalis* 26: 81–106.

Ibrahim Kunju, A. P. 2007. *Medieval Kerala.* Thiruvananthapuram: International Centre for Kerala Studies, University of Kerala.

—. 1975. *Mysore-Kerala Relations in the Eighteenth Century.* Trivandrum: Kerala Historical Society.

Innes, C. A. 1933. *Madras District Gazetteers. Malabar.* F. B. Evans (ed.). Madras: Government Press.

Jeffrey, R. 1992. *Politics, Women and Well-Being: How Kerala Became 'a Model'?.* London: The MacMilllan Press.

—. 1994. *The Decline of Nair Dominance. Society and Politics in Travancore, 1847–1908.* New Delhi: Manohar Publishers.

Kareem, C. K. 1973. *Kerala under Hyder Ali and Tipu Sultan.* Ernakulam: Cochin: Paico Publishing House.

Karwe, I. 1965. *Kinship Organization in India.* Bombay: Asia Publishing House.

Kintaert, T. 2005. *The Use of Primary Colours in the Nāṭyaśāstra.* In: S. Das and E. Fürlinger (eds). *Sāmarasya: Studies in Indian Arts, Philosophy and Interreligious Dialogue: in Honour of Bettina Bäumer.* New Delhi: D.K. Printworld: 245–273.

Kooiman, D. 1992. State Formation in Travancore: Problems of Revenue, Trade and Armament. In: A. W. van den Hoek et al. (ed.). *Ritual, State and History in South Asia: Essays in Honour of J. C. Heesterman.* Leiden: Brill: 587–609.

Krishna Iyer, L. A. 1968. *Social History of Kerala. Vol. 1, The pre-Dravidians.* Madras: Book Centre Publications.

—. 1970. *Social History of Kerala. Vol. 2, The Dravidians.* Madras: Book Centre Publications.

—. 1937. *The Travancore Tribes and Castes.* Vol. 1. Trivandrum: Government Press.

Krishna Ayyar, K. V. 1938. *The Zamorins of Calicut. From the Earliest Times down to CE 1806.* Calicut: The Norman Printing Bureau.

—. 1966. *A Short History of Kerala.* Ernakulam: Pai Company.

Krishna Menon, T. K. 1990. A Primer of Malayalam Literature. New Delhi Madras: Asian Educational Services.

Kunjunni Raja, K. 1980. *Contribution of Kerala to Sanskrit Literature.* Madras: University of Madras.

Kumar, U. 2010. Shaping a Literary Space: Early Literary Histories in Malayalam and Normative Uses of the Past. In: H. Harder (ed.). *Literature and Nationalist Ideology. Writing Histories of Modern Indian Languages,* New Delhi: Social Science Press: 19–50.

Kusuman, K. K. 1987. *A History of Trade Commerce in Travancore, 1600–1805.* Delhi: Mittal Publications.

Lienhard, S. 1984. *A History of Classical Poetry: Sanskrit-Pali-Prakrit. A History of Indian Literature. Vol. III, Classical Sanskrit literature.* Wiesbaden: Otto Harrassowitz.

Logan, W. 1981. *Malabar.* 2 Vols. Trivandrum: Charithram Press.

Madhava Menon T., et al. 2002. *People of India. Kerala. Anthropological Survey of India.* Vol. 27. Pt. 1–2. New Delhi: Affiliated East-West Press.

Maheswari, U. S. (ed.) 2015. *Sree Chithira Tirunal. Life and Times.* Thiruvananthapuram: Sri Uthradom Tirunal Marthanda Varma Literary and Charitable Trust.

Mailaparambil, B. J. 2011. *Lords of the Sea: The Ali Rajas of Cannanore and the Political Economy of Malabar (1663–1723).* Leiden: Brill.

Martin-Dubost, P. 1983. *Poèmes D'Amour du Kerala. XVe–XVIIe siècle.* Paris: Société D'Édition "Les Belles Lettres".

Mathew, K. S. 1979. *Society in Medieval Malabar. A Study Based on Vadakkaṅ Pāṭṭukaḷ.* Kottayam: Jaffe Books.

Meenu, B. 2016. Social Reform and the Gender Question: A Reading of Chathu Nair's *Meenakshi* (1890) in the Context of the 19th Century Debate Over Nair Caste Marriage. In: *Literary Quest* 2(10): 14–29.

Menon, V. K. R. 2005. *History of Medieval Kerala.* R. Ramachandran et al. (ed.). New Delhi: Pragati Publications.

Moser, H. 2011. *Bibliography of Kutiyattam.* https://publikationen.uni-tuebingen.de/xmlui/handle/10900/46921.

Moser, H. and P. Younger. 2013. Kerala: Plurality and Consensus. In: P. Berger and F. Heidemann (eds). *The Modern Anthropology of India. Etnography, Themes and Theory.* London New York: Routledge: 136–156.

Mukund, K. 1999. *Women's Property Rights in South India: A Review.* In: *Economic and Political Weekly* 34(22): 1352–1358.

Nagam Aiya, V. 1906. *The Travancore State Manual.* 3 Vols. Trivandrum: Government Press.

Nair, J. V. and K. S. Nair. 2001. Attingal: A Principality Reigned by Queens. In: A. R. Ramachandra Reddy (ed.). *Proceedings Volume of the Tenth Annual Session of South Indian History Congress.* India: General Secretary, South Indian History Congress: 82–87.

Nair, K. K. 2013. *By Sweat and Sword. Trade and War in Kerala through the Ages.* New Delhi: Manohar.

Narayanan, M. G. S. 1977. *Re-interpretations in South Indian History.* Trivandrum: College Book House.

—. 1996. *Perumals of Kerala. Political and Social Conditions of Kerala under Cēra Perumals of Makotai (c. 800 CE-1124 CE)*. Calicut: Xavier Press.

—. 2003. Historiography of Kerala: Some Important Issues. In: *Issues in Kerala Historiography*. K. K. Kusuman (ed.). Thiruvananthapuram: International Centre for Kerala Studies, University of Kerala: 192–201.

Narayana Pilliai, P. K. 1984. Introduction. In: Kēraḷavarmma. *The Peacock Messenger: Mayūradūtam: with an English Translation*. P. K. Narayana Pilliai (transl.). Trivandrum: 17–24.

Neumayer, E. and Ch. Schelberger (eds). 2005. *Raja Ravi Varma, Portrait of an Artist: The Diary of C. Raja Raja Varma*. New Delhi: Oxford University Press.

Nilakanta Sastri, K. A. 1929. *The Pāṇḍyan Kingdom: from the Earliest Times to the Sixteenth Century*. London, Luzac Co.

—. 2008. *A History of South India*. New Delhi: Oxford University Press.

Nisha, M. 2015. Making a Foray into the Uninhabited Grounds of Writing: Thottaikkat Ikkavamma's "Subhadrarjunam". In: *Literary Miscellany: An International Journal of Literary Studies* 4(1–2). https://www.academia.edu/29116224/Making_a_Foray_into_the_Uninhabited_Grounds_of_Writing_Thottaikkat_Ikkavammas_Subhadrarjunam.

Osella, F. and C. Osella. 2000. *Social Mobility in Kerala: Modernity and Identity in Conflict*. London-Sterling, Virginia: Pluto Press.

Padmanabha Menon, K. P. 1993. *History of Kerala Written in the Form of Notes on Visscher's Letters from Malabar*. Vol. 3. New Delhi: Asian Education Services.

Parpola, M. 2001. *Kerala Brahmins in Transition. A Study of a Nampūtiri Family.* Studia Orientalia 91. Helsinki: Finnish Oriental Society.

Pierdominici Leão, D. 2019. *Through the Eyes of a Warrior, Traveller and Poet: Portugal, Malabar and Indian Traditions as Seen by Luís Vaz de Camões (Os Lusíadas VII, 17–85).* In: *Cracow Indological Studies* 21(2): 159–178.

Pillai, M. S. 2015. *The Ivory Throne: Chronicles of the House of Travancore.* Noida: HarperCollins Publishers India.

Pomata, G. 1993. History, Particular and Universal. On Reading Some Recent Women's History Textbooks. In: *Feminists Studies* 19(1): 6–50. https://doi.org/10.2307/3178349.

Puri, T. 2018. For the Record: An Educational Memoir in Late Colonial India. In: *Cracow Indological Studies* 20(2): 47–70. https://doi.org/10.12797/cis.20.2018.02.04.

Raghava Varier, M. R. 2002. State as Svarūpam: An Introductory Essay. In: R. Champakalakshmy et al. (ed.). *State and Society in Pre-modern South India*, Thrissur: Cosmobooks: 120–130.

Raghavan, V. 1956. *Vijayanka, Vikatanitamba, Avantisundari. Three Sanskrit Prekshanakas.* Madras: Sri Ramachandra Printing Works.

—. 1964. Shakespeare in Sanskrit. In: *Indian Literature* 7(1): 109–114.

Raghunandan, L. 1995. *At the Turn of the Tide: the Life and Times of Maharani Setu Lakshmi Bayi, the Last Queen of Travancore.* Bangalore: Maharani Setu Lakshmi Bayi Memorial Charitable Trust.

Raja, P. K. S. 1953. *Mediaeval Kerala.* Chidambaram: Annamalai University.

Raja, P. K. R. V., Raja, P. A. G. V. 2017. *Oru "tīrthayātra" (A "Pilgrimage")*. Poonjar: Kanjiramattom Trust.

Raja, R. P. 2006. *New Light on Swathi Thirunal.* Trivandrum: Centre for Interdisciplinary Studies.

Rājā, Ar. Pi. (ed.). 2012. *Cemprōl Kōṭṭārattil Svāti Tirunāḻ Ambādēvi Tampurāṭṭi.* Kottayam: Kshatriya Kshemasabha Thiruvananthapuram.

Rājā, Ar. Pi. 2014. *Irayimman Tampi Kaviyum Kālavum.* Kottayam: Aryagayathri Publication.

Ramachandran Nair, K. 1997. Medieval Malayalam Literature. In: K. Ayyappa Paniker (ed.). *Medieval Indian Literature: 1. Surveys and selections.* New Delhi: Sahitya Akademi: 299–323.

Rāma Varma Rājā, Pi. Ar. 1988. *Pūññāṟ Rājakuṭumba Caritrāvalōkanam.* Poonjar: Poonjar Koyikkal Trust.

Rao, V. N. 2005. Purāṇa. In: S. Mittal and G. Thursby (eds). *The Hindu World.* New York–London: Routledge.

Ray, A. 2004. *The Merchant and the State: The French in India, 1666–1739.* Vol. 2. New Delhi: Munshiram Manoharlal Publishers.

Renou, L. 1959. Sur La Structure Du Kāvya. In: *Journal Asiatique*, tome CCXLVII: 1–114.

Sāmbaśiva Sāstrī, K. 1930. Preface. In: *Devarājakavi. The Bālamārtāndavijaya of Devarājakavi.* K. Sāmbaśiva Sāstrī (ed.). Trivandrum: Government Press: 1–12.

Sāmbaśiva Śāstrī, K. 1935. Introduction. In: K. Sāmbaśiva Śāstrī (ed.). *Bālarāmabharatam of Śrī Bālarāma Varma Vanci Maharaja.* Trivandrum: Government Press: 1–17.

Saradamoni, K. 1999. *Matriliny Transformed. Family, Law and Ideology in Twentieth Century Travancore.* New Delhi: Sage Publications and Altamira Press.

Sethuraman, N. 1980. *Medieval Pandyas (CE 1000–1200).* Kumbakonam: India: Raman and Raman.

Shah, Sh. 2017. Articulation, Dissent and Subversion: Voices of Women's Emancipation in Sanskrit Literature. In: *Social Scientist* 45(9–10): 79–86.

Shungoonny Menon, P. 1985. *A History of Travancore from the Earliest Times.* New Delhi: Asian Educational Services.

s'Jacob, H. K. 2001. *The Rajas of Cochin: 1663–1720: Kings, Chiefs, and the Dutch East India Company.* New Delhi: Munshiram Manoharlal Publishers.

Sreedhara Menon, A. (ed.). 1962. *Kerala District Gazetteers: Trivandrum.* Trivandrum: Government Press.

—. 1962. *Kerala District Gazetteers: Kozhikode.* Trivandrum: Government Press.

—. 2014. *A Survey of Kerala History.* Kottayam: DC Books.

Staal, J. F. 1961. *Nambudiri Veda Recitation.* The Hague: Mouton Co.

—. 1983. *Agni. The Vedic Ritual of the Fire Altar.* 2 Vols. Berkeley: Asian Humanities Press.

Sternbach, L. 1974. *A History of Indian Literature. Vol. 4, Scientific and Technical Literature, Fasc. 1, Subhāṣita, Gnomic and Didactic Literature.* J. Gonda (ed.). Wiesbaden: Harrassowitz.

Subramanian, K. H. 2008. *Kerala Panini and Sanskrit Works.* Delhi: New Bharatiya Book Corporation.

Sudyka, J. 2014. *The Iron Age Culture and Settlement in South India*. Saarbrücken: Lambert Academic Publishing.

Sudyka, L. 2011. *Ucchvāsa, sarga* and *lambha*: Text Divisions in Sanskrit Poems (*mahākāvyas*). In: *Cracow Indological Studies* 13: 15–39.

—. 2013. *Vijayanagara: A Forgotten Empire of Poetesses. Part I. The Voice of Gaṅgādevī*. Kraków: Ksiegarnia Akademicka.

—. 2016. Zapomniana poezja. Sanskrycka twórczość kobiet z rodu władców Koczinu. In: *Przeglad Orientalistyczny* 1–2(257–258): 217–230.

—. 2018a. Kerala Women's Writing in Sanskrit. Ambādevi Tampurāṭṭi of Cemprol Koṭṭāraṁ: Her Life and Literary Oeuvre. In: *Rocznik Orientalistyczny* 71(2): 187–197.

—. 2018b. The "Santānagopāla" as a Narrative Opening up Intimate Spaces. Lakṣmī Tampurāṭṭi and Her Poem. In: *Cracow Indological Studies* 20(2): Opening up Intimate Spaces: Women's Writing, Autobiography and Biography in South Asia: 71–87. https://doi.org/10.12797/cis.20.2018.02.05.

—. 2019 In Search of Women's Sanskrit Writings in Kerala. In: *Rivista degli Studi Orientali*: 127–142.

Schildt, H. 2012. *The Traditional Kerala Manor: Architecture of a South Indian Catuḥśāla House*. Pondicherry: Institut Français de Pondicherry & École française d'Extrême-Orient.

Sundaram Pillai, P. 1986. *Some Early Sovereigns of Travancore*. Madras: Pionier Book Services.

Szczepanik, L. 2015. *Come Fly with Me. Messengers in Indian Skies. A Study of Sanskrit dūtakāvya Poetry with Reference to the Vāgmaṇḍanaguṇadūtakāvya of Vireśvara*. Unpublished Ph.D. thesis. Kraków: Jagiellonian University.

Tharakan, M. 1984. Socio-Economic Factors in Educational Development: Case of Nineteenth Century Travancore. In: *Economic and Political Weekly* 19(46): 1959–1967.

Tharu, S. 2013. *Foreword.* In: Chandumenon. *Indulekha.* A. Devasia (transl.). New Delhi: Oxford University Press: IX-XI.

Tharu, S. and K. Lalita. 1991. *Women Writing in India. 600 B.C. to the Present. Vol. 1: 600 B.C. to the Early Twentieth Century.* Delhi: Oxford University Press.

Thurston, E. and K. Rangachari. 1909. *Castes and Tribes of Southern India.* Vol. 4. Madras: Government Press.

Tieken, H. 1993. The So-Called Trivandrum Plays Attributed to Bhāsa. In: *Vienna Journal of South Asian Studies* 37: 5–44.

—. 1997. Three Men in a Row. (Studies in the Trivandrum Plays II). In: *Wiener Zeitschrift Für Die Kunde Südasiens und Archiv Für Indische Philosophie* 41: 17–52.

—. 2013. Daṇḍin, the "Daśakumāracarita", and the "Avantisundarīkathā". In: *Bulletin d'Études Indiennes* 31: 231–252.

Unni, N. P. 1995. *Nilakantha Diksita.* New Delhi: Sahitya Akademi.

Unithiri, N. V. P. 2004. *Studies in Kerala Sanskrit Literature.* Calicut: Publication Division University of Calicut.

Ulloor S. Parameswara Iyer, *Essays on Travancore*, Cultural Publications Department, Government of Kerala, Thiruvananthapuram 2003.

Uḷḷūr [= Uḷḷūr Sa. Paramēśvarayyar]. 1990. *Kēraḷasāhityacaritṟaṃ*, vol. V, Trivandrum: Kerala University.

Uyl den, M. 1995. *Invisible Barriers. Gender, Caste and Kinship in a Southern Indian Village.* Utrecht: International Books.

Vaidyanathan, K. R. 1982. *Temples and Legends of Kerala*. Bombay: Bharatiya Vidya Bhavan.

Varghese, G. 2018. Socio-Cultural Studies of Tribal Communities of Kerala. In: *Advance Research Journal of Multidisciplinary Discoveries* 24(6): 45–49.

Vielle, Ch. 2012. Ravivarman Kulaśekhara the Yādava and Sagara the Son of Yādavī: Real and Ideal Kings in Matrilineal Kerala. In: *Religions of South Asia* 5(1): 365–387.

—. 2014. How did Paraśurāma Come to Raise Kerala? In: Kesavan Veluthat. D. R. Davis, Jr. (ed.). *Irreverent History. Essays for M. G. S. Narayanan*. Delhi: Primus Books: 15–32.

Venkatasubramonia Iyer, S. 1976. *Kerala Sanskrit Literature. A Bibliography*. Trivandrum: Department of Sanskrit, University of Kerala.

Viswanathan Peterson, I. 2003. *Design and Rhetoric in a Sanskrit Court Epic. The "Kiratārjunīya" of Bhāravi*. Albany: State University of New York Press.

Warder, A. K. 1983. *Indian Kāvya Literature. Vol. 4. The Ways of Originality (Bāṇa to Dāmodaragupta)*. Delhi: Motilal Banarsidass.

Wigram, H. 1882. *A Commentary on Malabar Law and Custom*. Madras: Graves, Cookson and Co.

Wood, A. E. 1985. *Knowledge before Printing and after. The Indian Tradition in Changing Kerala*. Delhi–New York: Oxford University Press.

Wójcik, A. Bālarāmabharata" of Kartika Tirunal Balarama Varma: the Patronage of the Rajahs of Travancore (forthcoming).

Zarrilli, P. B. 1994. An Ocean of Possibilities: From "Lokadharmī to Nāṭyadharmī" in a "Kathakali Santānagopālam". In: *Comparative Drama* 28(1): 67–89. https://doi.org/10.1353/cdr.1994.0003.

—. 2000. *Kathakali Dance-Drama: Where Gods and Demons Come to Play*. London–New York: Routledge.

—. 2007. Kathakaḷi. In: F. P. Richmond et al. (ed.) *Indian Theatre. Traditions of Performance*. Delhi: Motilal Banarsidass Publishers: 315–358.

—. 2010. *When the Body Becomes All Eyes: Paradigms, Discourses and Practices of Power in Kalarippayattu, a South Indian Martial Art*. New Delhi–Oxford: Oxford University Press.

Index of Kerala Sanskrit Authoresses' Names